Call Me MISTER

Call Me MISTER

The Re-Emergence of African American Male Teachers in South Carolina

ROY JONES & ARETTA JENKINS

Copyright © 2012 by Roy Jones & Aretta Jenkins

All rights reserved. No part of this book may be used or reproduced in any manner whatsoever without prior written consent of the author, except as provided by the United States of America copyright law.

Published by Advantage, Charleston, South Carolina.
Member of Advantage Media Group.

ADVANTAGE is a registered trademark and the Advantage colophon is a trademark of Advantage Media Group, Inc.

Printed in the United States of America.

ISBN: 978-159932-339-8
LCCN: 2012955098

This publication is designed to provide accurate and authoritative information in regard to the subject matter covered. It is sold with the understanding that the publisher is not engaged in rendering legal, accounting, or other professional services. If legal advice or other expert assistance is required, the services of a competent professional person should be sought.

Advantage Media Group is proud to be a part of the Tree Neutral® program. Tree Neutral offsets the number of trees consumed in the production and printing of this book by taking proactive steps such as planting trees in direct proportion to the number of trees used to print books. To learn more about Tree Neutral, please visit www.treeneutral.com. To learn more about Advantage's commitment to being a responsible steward of the environment, please visit www.advantagefamily.com/green

Advantage Media Group is a leading publisher of business, motivation, and self-help authors. Do you have a manuscript or book idea that you would like to have considered for publication? Please visit www.advantagefamily.com or call 1.866.775.1696

To the elders, those black men and women, throughout history, who dared to dream, prayed and stayed the course in the long, continuous fight for the right (privilege) to learn.

To the Misters, who were called into service, to set the example and lead the way, as a beacon of light for generations to follow. And, to the countless number of black boys, who have to endure enormous hardships and overcome the odds operating against their success.

SPECIAL THANKS:
Shiloh Baptist Church for allowing access to the historic Shiloh School

COVER PHOTOGRAPHER:
Patrick Wright

COVER PHOTO:
Mister Mark Joseph (left)
Mister Hayward Jean (center)
Mister Justin Ballenger (right)

COVER BACKGROUND:
The Shiloh (Queensdale) Elementary School (circa 1929-30) built for Negro children with funding support from the Negro community ($1,000); public sources ($1,400) and the Rosenwald Fund ($500).
Source: Fisk University Rosenwald Fund Card File Data Base

Special Acknowledgements

To the original presidents, whose institutional leadership, commitment and collaboration made it possible for Call Me MISTER to plant its seed and germinate for more than a decade in South Carolina.

> James Barker, *President, Clemson University*
> Luns Richardson, *President, Morris College*
> David Swinton, *President, Benedict College*
> Henry Tisdale, *President, Claflin University*

To these men for their vision, determination, advocacy and faith in the idea that young black men could change the course of history by standing at the head of the class.

> Harold Cheatham, *Dean, Emeritus*
> Tom Parks, *Professor, Emeritus*
> Jeff "The Judge" Davis, *Member 1981 Clemson National Championship Football Team & College Football Hall of Fame Inductee*

Personal Thanks

To my mother and to the memory of my father Beverly and Bobby Jenkins, whose stability, strength and determination made it possible for me to live and strive in South Carolina.

To the memory of my father, Joseph Jones and my mother, Elizabeth Jones Goodwin, who instilled in me my principles, sense of integrity, a strong work ethic and desire for an education, while sacrificing and persevering to raise us right.

To Gladys Machen, my "renaissance" grandmother, whose lesson on living off the land greatly contributes to my philosophy.

To my great aunt Pearl Underwood and my great uncle Andy Machen, whose generational knowledge on our family economics and politics grounded my lesson in history. And, to my grandfather, Perry Jenkins, a respected South Carolina farmer, who left me with a foundation.

To the little girls, Gingerlynn and Jessah Jenkins, who grew up going from porch to porch gathering oral histories with momma.

Table of Contents

About the Authors..................................15
Foreword: *A World of Difference by Winston Holton* 19
Introduction: *A Harvest of Hope* 25

PART 1: THE ROOTS OF A CRISIS

Chapter 1: *The Persistence of Stereotypes* 43
Chapter 2: *The Drain of Social Problems* 53
Chapter 3: *The Evolution of the Issues* 65

PART 2: OPPORTUNITY FOR NEW GROWTH

Chapter 1: *The Mission of Call Me MISTER* 95
Chapter 2: *The Early Days* 107
Chapter 3: *How the Program Works*..................113

PART 3: SPREADING THE SEEDS

Chapter 1: *Reaping What We Sow* 125
Chapter 2: *The Vision Widens* 131
Chapter 3: *Where Next?*............................135
Conclusion: *"Teamwork Makes the Dream Work"* 141

The Call Me MISTER Blazer

The Call Me MISTER Blazer symbolizes supreme achievement. It is presented to each Mister who has completed an academic program that has prepared him for a teaching credential. It is presented to each Mister who has met the ideals and objectives of the program's co-curriculum, which include strong personal development, empowerment, leadership, responsibility, service, and focus on success principles.

The Blazer honors the Mister's persistence, dedication, commitment, and endurance. The Blazer, which should be worn with great pride, carries with it the enormous responsibility of acting as a role model for others, especially young people. The Blazer represents the value of achieving a goal. This highest honor—the beautiful black Blazer with its fancy buttons and trademark Call Me MISTER logo on the breast pocket—is presented during an investiture ceremony each summer. Receiving the Blazer is tantamount to winning the Green Jacket at the Masters Golf Tournament in Augusta, but with far greater significance. The Blazer takes four years, not four days, to earn.

Receiving the Blazer also symbolizes the beginning of a journey for each Mister. We ask each Mister to wear it the first day he enters the classroom as a new teacher and on the last day of that first teaching year. He also can wear it at other times, at his discretion, to represent the Call Me MISTER program. The Blazer represents the pride that we want every Mister to feel.

ABOUT THE AUTHORS

DR. ROY JONES is Executive Director of Clemson University's Eugene T. Moore School of Education's Call Me MISTER (Mentors Instructing Students Toward Effective Role Models) program and Associate Professor in the department of Educational Leadership. The program's goal is to place more teachers from diverse cultures and backgrounds in the classrooms of low-performing elementary schools. The program has been remarkably successful in recruiting and developing African American males to serve as teachers in South Carolina's public school classrooms. *Diverse Issues in Higher Education* selected the program as one of its top ten Diversity Champions.

A lifelong educator, Jones has effectively implemented and directed numerous programs in higher education. He is often sought as a speaker and has presented workshops, seminars, forums, and panel discussions on racial and cultural issues in education to a wide range of audiences.

Jones received his doctorate from the University of Georgia, his master's degree from Atlanta University, and his bachelor's degree from the University of Massachusetts, Amherst. In 2009, Jones received the American Association of Blacks in Higher Education's Pacesetter Award.

ARETTA JENKINS has been an oral historian for years. She founded CornBread Chronicles, LLC, a South Carolina company specializing in preserving the legacy and journey of agrarian life in the Upstate. A Clemson graduate who majored in history and women's studies, she produced a widely distributed documentary about the Call Me MISTER program that depicted the lives of several of the young men. She continues to provide marketing strategies including recorded interviews with major funders, students, and presidents of partner colleges.

She was one of the earliest African American pioneers to host a radio show on Atlanta's historic station 750 WSB and has hosted her own shows on a variety of stations. She has been a popular mistress of ceremonies and voice artist for most of her career.

Jenkins has served as a public elementary school certified parent educator and received the WYFF 4 Golden Apple Award. An adult-education teacher, she was recognized by the Department of Social Services for retaining the largest number of adult learners in class toward completion, based upon a statewide comparison.

In Dr. Jones' words, here is how he and Jenkins combined their unique abilities to advance the program and write this book:

"Several years ago, Aretta and I met, and she advised me about how Call Me MISTER could more effectively market its brand to attract program support. Her deep-seated interest in capturing oral histories and family backgrounds naturally led her toward developing the idea of documenting the journeys of our young men. The first major project was the South Carolina ETV documentary, which conveyed the importance our program places on the lives and backgrounds of the population we serve. Our tenth anniversary commemoration in 2010 also highlighted the program's collective journey and growth. As a practitioner administering the day-to-day dynamic development of the program, I would have found it virtually impossible to write a book. Aretta made it possible, in large measure, with her encouragement and dedication to 'telling the story': a South Carolina story. The voices in the book speak for themselves—the rest of us just did our part. We spent a year searching for just the right publisher who could understand our mission and show us a way to make it happen, and here we are!"

To learn more about *Call Me MISTER*:

E-mail: MISTER@clemson.edu

Phone: 1-800-640-2657 (toll-free)

Mail:
  Call Me MISTER
  203 Holtzendorff Clemson University
  Clemson, SC 29634

Website: www.callmemister.clemson.edu

Inquiries and applications for admission are open to anybody, regardless of race, color, ethnicity, gender, age, or religion, who can help the program achieve its objectives.

I saw the angel in the marble and carved until I set him free.

—MICHELANGELO

FOREWORD

A World of Difference

No program endeavoring to develop African American males embraces the challenge of honoring, respecting, and, I dare say, safeguarding difference as Call Me MISTER does. Many other programs disdain the individual, and specifically seek, by the nature of their indoctrination exercises, to tear people down with the intent of rebuilding them in some predetermined image to meet an often narrowly focused purpose. Call Me MISTER rebukes this deconstruct-to-reconstruct model and embraces a far more aggrandizing paradigm. We believe in the innate genius of every Mister—or to paraphrase Michelangelo, we believe a beautiful sculpture exists in every block of stone—and it is our privilege and challenge to reveal it. This is done through a prescriptive, guided process of self-analysis that leads to a heightened state of self-efficacy by which each Mister actually sees himself capable of wresting positive outcomes from difficult situations.

The current narrative of the African American male too often focuses on deficits, and, in response, many employ shortsighted, reconstructionist models to predictably limited corrective success. Contained within these narratives, in the midst of the dysfunction, miseducation, and tragedy, is the stuff of legends. Misters learn to embrace their stories—you hear this so vibrantly in their testimonies. Rather than being embarrassing tomes, their stories are empowering anthems rallying others to greatness. This relentless, unapologetic belief in the inherent value of each of the young men in our charge fuels our transformative process. This predilection allows us to see through the distractions of unfortunate circumstance by acknowledging existing problems without denigrating the young men as actually embodying those problems. No two Misters are the same; accordingly, no two Misters are treated exactly the same.

Any intervening strategy must accommodate this reality. In current educational parlance, this is known as instituting an individualized education plan (IEP); Call Me MISTER alters this slightly and creates an individualized *empowerment* plan for each of our participants.

We value and honor diversity, as evidenced by the myriad of philosophical underpinnings, pedagogical approaches, and teaching styles masterfully demonstrated by our graduates. There is no prototypical Mister; our young men run the gamut of socio-economic, religious, political, and, yes, ethnic backgrounds. Misters share a singular mission, vision, and purpose, but they are not the same. That, as people say, makes all the difference.

We must also consider what will make the difference for our schools. There is a very good reason why educational and political pundits cannot agree upon which technological innovation, philosophical approach, or general educational course would truly lead to the overall betterment of South Carolina schools—there is not just one. Thus, the confusion results less from discerning between the relative values of a kaleidoscope of disparate possibilities and more from the misguided premise that there is but one solution to this educational quagmire.

Call Me MISTER does not make this mistake. We expose our young men to a vibrant spectrum of ideas and allow each to choose the one that best suits his ideological palette. It is not uncommon for Drs. Jawanza Kunjufu and Abigail Thernstrom to find themselves on the same dais addressing an audience of Misters. Having Misters listen firsthand to former Governor Jeb Bush discuss his education reform initiatives in Florida, or to former U.S. Secretary of Education and South Carolina Governor Richard Riley reflect on his hallowed career, expands their horizons as well. While Misters are given latitude to discern which methods align best with their personal philosophies, beliefs, and talents, understand that arriving at these determinations is not a capricious process; one of the primary aims of the Call Me MISTER co-curricular process is to develop and hone the critical thinking skills that are the cornerstone of effective decision making.

Education is a profession that suffers no shortage of ideologues; our practice is to provide opportunity for Misters to debrief collectively soon after these experiences. We challenge Misters to analyze different theoretical approaches through several lenses via facilitated sessions, which are sometimes formal (breakout sessions, small group meetings, weekly seminars, etc.) and many times informal (commutes, texting, phone calls, prompt meals, etc.). We encourage Misters to develop one more traditional focus by illuminating and evaluating the general merits, strengths, and weaknesses of these theoretical approaches. As their understanding of Call Me MISTER matures, the Misters' appraisals become driven by the tenets of servant leadership, social justice, and community revitalization. This last and most crucial tenet requires each Mister to assess how well a given approach melds with his evolving educational philosophy. Each cohort of Misters provides a wonderful cocoon for the incubation of each Mister's ideas and beliefs about two concepts: first, who he is as an educator; second, how his passion and drive will best manifest themselves professionally and personally.

Theory is good. Practice is better. We place Misters in front of children right away, often before they have taken their first official educational course. They must know early that working with young people is their calling. Veteran, credentialed Misters guide the initiate Misters in our program's tenets by delivering valuable tutelage and mentoring to young people in the community. Through internships, community engagement initiatives, and school-based outreach, our initiate Misters secure early indoctrination into the mission and vision of Call Me MISTER. As a result, theory is no longer "theoretical"; instead, it is the foundation for more highly effective practice. Doctors and lawyers practice until retirement—people in these professions possess the foundational belief that an artisan can always be better and there is always a greater ideal to be reached. Misters understand this. There is no such thing as a *pre*-service Mister—they are always *in*-service. We engage them immediately. Rather than simply creating isolated opportunities for advancement, we work to nurture relational networks in which growth and development are de facto benefits of membership. Participation in this process is also why Misters do not leave the profession.

Finally, Call Me MISTER has adopted the altruistic slogan "Teamwork Makes the Dream Work" as a guiding principle. This principle serves to remind us that we do not exist in a vacuum; moreover, we have tremendously talented human resources in our schools and communities with whom we need to connect. Robert K. Greenleaf, commonly credited with coining the term "servant leader," opined that one must practice service endeavors in a manner that encourages and fosters other like-minded individuals. South Carolina schools remain microcosms of the communities in which they are found. Unfortunately, our communities are ailing in vast numbers. If it takes a village to raise a child, what then does the reality of the state of our villages portend for our children? More than mere teachers, Misters are architects. They build villages.

—Winston Holton
Call Me MISTER field coordinator, Clemson University

*Not everything that counts can be measured,
and not everything that can be measured counts.*

–ALBERT EINSTEIN (ATTRIBUTED)

INTRODUCTION

A Harvest of Hope

Over the past dozen years, whenever we have spoken with educators, elected officials, or potential benefactors about Call Me MISTER, we have found that our conversations rise to a whole new level when the young men in the program come with us. When they tell their stories, hearts change.

Few would deny that our public schools are in crisis. While this is an American problem, it is particularly acute in the South. In South Carolina, where Call Me MISTER was founded, we know the issues all too well. Schools are suffering from low performance and low achievement—and when the schools are poor in quality, so are many of those who teach in them.

We hear loud demands for alternatives, particularly from communities in which pockets of the very poor live amid pockets of the very wealthy. That is why tuition tax credit and other school choice alternatives to attend private schools are popular. These and other choice options provide an escape from all the trappings associated with poverty and low-performing public schools, at public expense.

Call Me MISTER strives to improve the quality of instruction with an alternative model for teacher preparation that will truly make a difference. The program—founded at Clemson University, along with its original partners, the three historically black institutions of Benedict College, Claflin University, and Morris College—gets to the heart of the issues by recruiting, developing, and placing strong, motivated teachers. Specifically, Call Me MISTER seeks out capable African American men who can reach out to children who need positive role models and dedicated mentors, thereby elevating the schools' culture.

We develop the men in our program—we call them "Misters"—to recognize the value in building healthy relationships with their students and seeing those students in the context of their lives. We believe such relationships can raise academic achievement. Such a relationship compensates for a student's low self-esteem, low confidence, low expectations, destructive behaviors, and bad habits. The program spends a great deal of time and attention in developing this dimension in Misters.

Call Me MISTER equips these men to help the often-troubled communities in which far too many children live. Many Misters came from similar backgrounds, even from those very same places. We ask them to return to their communities and serve in the elementary and middle schools. This return is a critical step. If we equip a corps of young teachers who are committed to taking on tough assignments, we can make a difference for individual pupils, their schools, and even entire communities.

Hearing about the journeys of those who have been through the program seems to touch our audiences' souls. The grim storyline of education has seemed only to get worse, and people want solutions. They want to support a cause that will do something. When children can see that teaching is respectable employment for a black man, they well might aspire to be teachers themselves. Through our program, we plant the seeds for a new crop of educators.

RECAPTURING PRIDE AND RESPECT

One of the motivations for our program came from the goal of destroying the stereotypical images of black males as criminals, dealers, and hustlers. We wanted to bring to light the true attributes, virtues, and creativity of black males that so seldom are portrayed.

In 2007, we created a documentary about the young men in Call Me MISTER that told their story—much of it in their own words. The documentary captured the program's essence. In the documentary, produced by this book's coauthor, Aretta Jenkins, we went to the towns where the Misters had grown up. We went down the dirt driveways. We visited their grandparents. We portrayed the world that many of the Call Me MISTER teachers called home—and to which many of them have returned to do their part for change.

What we found in visiting these homes were the old-school values and principles that produce men of honor, despite long-standing issues of poverty and segregation. These men were well grounded in family and community.

Pride and respect is what we are trying to recapture. We want to build a value system that will uplift these young men and their families and communities. Such dignity has long defined black culture. Even under the oppression of the Jim Crow era, for example, when African Americans might have held their heads down when passing a white man on the street, they held their heads high in their own homes and churches; they lived in an atmosphere of respect.

Over the past few generations, however, unmistakable social trends have continued to deeply influence African American communities in the South, and integration itself has led to profound change. We have witnessed the weakening of extended family and neighborhood bonds since the 1970s, along with the loss of the self-sufficiency mindset.

A STORY THAT MUST BE TOLD

There is a story that must be told now—a story of unity, community, and strong men and women. We see little of this story in our history books, and African American children have not understood it. This is a narrative that our youth are missing. As a result, they are losing touch with their identity and with the very sense of their roots and of who they are. They only go back as far as yesterday. To make matters worse, most schools feed them only commercial, sanitized versions of black heroes and heroines.

Previous generations of African Americans grew up with an oral tradition from which they learned those values. They knew their elders. If you ask a classroom of children today how many know their grandmother or grandfather, much less their great-grandparents, few will answer in the affirmative. Frequently, the authors have observed this trend during school visits at which we address student audiences. We see a disconnect between the generations, and we are trying to bridge that through this program. This assertion may sound odd to a reader from another race or culture, yet it is quite understandable, given the unique history of the African-in-America experience.

The Call Me MISTER program is firmly grounded in its historical context, which is one of a self-sufficient people. Many of these people were farmers or craftsmen who sustained themselves on what they could produce and build. Such was the cultural context that produced Benjamin E. Mays and Mary McLeod Bethune, two great educators of our time from South Carolina. Such was the cultural context of ordinary folks in Clarendon County, S.C., who envisioned and fought for a better future for generations of their children.

Most people know the narrative of America's change from its agrarian past—they know that many Americans, both white and black, once made their living off the land. While African American youth are taught that aspect of history, seldom does their education focus on the stability of their forebears' culture or on those forebears' principles and tough resolve.

Young people would be proud to hear that story, if only it were told. They would gain a sense of value from knowing they had descended from fine, strong, and savvy people. This knowledge can change the way people see the world; it nurtures respectful behavior.

African Americans have endured some horrific times, indeed. Yet, what Call Me MISTER does is the opposite of dwelling on the nightmares. It embraces the dreams. Even at the height of oppression, black men and women and their elders kept a space in their hearts and souls, where they knew themselves as people of dignity. They had a value system, and they protected themselves and their youth.

TAPPING A GREAT POTENTIAL

In sharing their own, individual stories, the men of Call Me MISTER likewise can effect change. Does one Mister make a difference? Yes. Do we expect that one Mister can transform a community? Yes, we can expect it; realistically, though, change takes time, and this is a tall, if not impossible, order. By empowering and effectively preparing young teachers, however, we can begin to face the challenge. These teachers can provide a powerful antidote to the ills in the schools.

Empowerment comes from within these individuals. It was there all along; we simply help to draw it out. The prospective teachers go to college and receive the requisite formal training. In addition, we recognize their special mission and provide them with what it will take to make that difference.

Call Me MISTER taps a great potential. The program sets specific standards for identifying and recruiting prospective teachers, and it works to ensure that our schools retain African American teachers, where those teachers are needed. Before placing the Misters in elementary and middle schools, the program develops them personally and professionally to both serve and lead, fulfilling a dire need in many townships.

It is this co-curricular developmental approach—the process of "Misterization"—that separates our program from other preparatory teaching programs. Each recruit understands what the program expects of him personally and professionally. The Misters become servant leaders dedicated to building community. They become highly effective, competent teachers able to meet children's instructional needs. They recognize they are being called upon to meet a special challenge at this critical stage in our country's history. This is a challenge not for the faint of heart.

To accomplish those goals, the Misters need the right disposition, mindset, and attitude. We help them to develop those values and strengthen their fortitude to do the work, day in and day out, and often night in and night out. Prospective teachers come to the program having experienced some of the same social ills that they will be working to cure. Many of them have been able to overcome their backgrounds, which is how they came our way. However, these men are the exception, not the rule. Many come to us with heavy personal baggage that is far more burdensome then what they should reasonably have at their age. Call Me MISTER meets these men where they are and begins building trust that is so essential if we expect growth and development.

In fact, any black male in college is an exception to the rule. Yet, we know what the Misters have inside of them. They have character. They have heart. They have been persistent and tough-minded. They have had faith that they can succeed. What they need most is mentoring, guidance, and support.

A WORLD OF CHANGE

South Carolina is made up of many small communities and a few larger towns and cities. While most of South Carolina is rural, the population is concentrated in a few urban areas: Greenville, Columbia, Charleston, Florence, and Spartanburg.

According to *African-American Historic Places in South Carolina*, published by the State Historic Preservation Office, about half of the U.S. population of African Americans have ties to South Carolina. During the days of slavery, the state's black population grew rapidly; by 1720, it was twice the state's white population.

Tourism has become the state's biggest industry, but for many, employment opportunity is limited. While South Carolina desperately struggles to attract large manufacturers, smaller rural towns are left out of the loop. In towns such as Estill, many people have to commute to their jobs in Hilton Head. That means an hour and a half of travel each way, by bus, for low-pay domestic service, janitorial work, or hotel employment. People in Estill jump on a bus before dawn to get to the tourism center, and they return home late in the evening. They are the groundskeepers and housekeepers for people who come to vacation or retire in South Carolina.

To support themselves, these laborers have to find work far away from their homes. Textile mills long sustained many communities, and such was the case in Estill. In many families, both parents worked at a plant, as did generations before them. However, the mills are gone, now, and the train does not run through Estill any more—nor does it run through many other rural communities.

As opportunity vanishes, so do people with dreams, visions, and expectations. Nothing remains to sustain them or their families. When Charleston's Navy base shut down, the source of livelihood for generations in the region had depended on vanished. These people had never dreamed their source of income would go away. No amount of forewarning could have eased the brutality of such a loss to so many families. The lack of employment rippled through the economy. What would all those people do? What employer would be able to pick up the thousands, who still needed to support their families?

In that context, how does a seventeen- or eighteen-year-old black male fit in? So much is written about what happens on Wall Street and how it affects people's lives. There is less insight into the nuances of what happens off Main Street in small-town America, especially in the rural South.

Once, when times were hard and jobs were scarce, nobody starved. They were able to grow their own food. They could heat their homes. They lived off the land. However, in so many communities, as the elders have passed away, land ownership has diminished. The homestead gave them a sense of stability. What happens when that land and opportunity are no longer there?

THE FLIGHT OF THE BRIGHT AND AMBITIOUS

That is when people feel the real squeeze. That is when young people not only flee their towns, but also flee their states: They go off to Atlanta, Baltimore, or Chicago. Often, those who flee are the brightest and most ambitious. For well over a generation, that trend has worsened as young people have left their hometowns in search of a better life. Often, they leave behind the most vulnerable members of their black communities: the elderly, the women, and the underemployed. Though we now have evidence that African Americans are migrating back to the South, the bottom line is this: Black communities in South Carolina have taken a severe blow.

Since World War II, small communities have felt the shift. Industrial bases shut down, and people went off in search of opportunities. While extended families had supported one another once, now many of those relatives had departed. The most creative minds moved elsewhere, and blight settled in.

Those of us who lived through that upheaval know it was so gradual that we did not grasp the implications. We hardly knew what was happening. Yet a lot of us were on that train. We would even encourage others: "Get out while you can." We never stopped to think about what we were leaving behind or whether we should fight for it.

THE BLIGHT LEFT BEHIND

People were disappearing. By the late 1980s and '90s, the shift was in full force. Those left behind felt a sense of abandonment. The drain of so many good souls not only weakened families, but also left an imbalance in communities.

Without a supply of future leaders, communities became vulnerable. The same people who were capable of fleeing were those who also were capable of helping their communities the most. However, they had lost any desire or opportunity to stay. Those who were left behind leaned on things that would relieve them of their pain. Once, rampant drug issues, alcoholism, and sexually transmitted diseases were almost unheard of in our communities. Now they are common, even among the elders, to whom young people should be looking for guidance. The sense of loss left people with such deep pain that they sought relief by destructive means. People who are cut off or isolated—people who lack the support of others who would catch them and keep them anchored—tend to make poor decisions.

This imbalance grew as the talent continued to flee. Some young people went off to college or joined the military. Many other rural youth throughout the South migrated to urban centers, such as Charlotte or Atlanta, for low-paying jobs. Many were not really equipped to move, so they wound up with new challenges, even if their challenges were limited to the struggle to pay their rent. Cut off from family support, they had to survive. They, too, became vulnerable—and the trend has continued.

A BLOW TO EDUCATION

The drain of creativity and leadership was particularly hard on the schools, since good prospective teachers were among those who left.

The young people who remained might have stepped forward to fill the gap in skills and talent, but they lacked role models, now that so many of the ambitious had left.

Many of the schools are as blighted as the rest of the communities because they have not been maintained or rebuilt. They depend on the local property tax base. Without a sound economy, and without a healthy middle class, a school system cannot thrive. These communities have lost the black middle class, the members of which could be their advocates for re-growth. Those who left are the people who would have served on the school boards. They would have been the local elected leaders and decision-makers. Having moved away, they have no influence on their hometowns.

Such a migration raises several questions: Who will become the teachers? Who will become the administrators? Who will run the schools?

African Americans continue to make up a significant proportion of the population—in many areas, a dominant proportion. In some areas, the number is 20 percent; in others, it is 50 percent and higher. The group has representation in numbers, but we still must ask: What difference does it make if the majority of a community's decision-makers are black, yet performance and achievement remain low and young people still lack opportunities after finishing school (if they finish school at all)?

Call Me MISTER teachers are at the cutting edge of a new crusade, to ensure quality education for black children by creating a pool of talented teachers, who are loyal to their communities. Such teachers embody the spirit of hope for change that this book embraces.

A TOUGH CHALLENGE

This is the challenge we give to the Misters who come from those small communities: Get your education and training, get your certificate and degree, and go back to your community and get to work lifting up the generations coming behind you. This homegrown model and philosophy is dedicated to the power of human investment in the development of these communities.

The program has its challenges. Affordable housing is hard to find, for example—so where are the teachers going to live? Some communities have mobile homes, and some have subsidized apartments, but not enough. Commuting great distances on a tight budget gets old quickly, and adequate public transportation is rare in such places.

If an idealistic college graduate, at twenty-two or twenty-three years old, has to commute 50 miles, how long should we expect that arrangement to last? No matter how dedicated that individual is to a mission, the logistics are daunting. If prospective teachers are not returning to the land and homes that their families own, how can we persuade them to move from Columbia, Charleston, or Greenville to work in places such as Estill? They have nowhere to live, and they are not part of that landscape, culture, or lifestyle.

Those communities still have value. The schools are not going to shut down, not as long as a population exists. They are still pumping along, ushering kids from kindergarten right on through twelfth grade. Yet, finding and retaining highly effective teachers is an ever-increasing challenge. Communities small and large have this struggle. The Charleston County School District, for example, has difficulty placing quality teachers—not necessarily in its metropolitan area, but in the county's outlying rural areas.

Hoping to find certified African American men who can excel as teachers in the lower grades has been like shooting for the moon.

The eligible teacher pool simply has not existed. When Call Me MISTER began, the naysayers predicted we would find no more than a few young men, who would want to teach third-graders. People wondered how many eighteen-year-olds would aspire to such a career, since teaching jobs were dominated by women in general and white women in particular, regardless of the student demographic. In our communities, there are no billboards or school rallies encouraging black males to become kindergarten teachers, which is precisely what is needed.

The Call Me MISTER graduates, however, have risen to the challenge. Life has prepared them well. They know what it is like in these schools and communities. Deep down, they feel a desire to be part of a badly needed change. We help them understand what they can do about how they feel. We encourage their personal development, creativity, and inherent sensitivity. Such encouragement is a huge part of what the program is all about.

Recruitment for Call Me MISTER has never been a problem, not since day one. We have found eager young men, who were ready to make a change. If anything could debunk certain assumptions about black males, these young men's interest in the program did so immediately. As soon as we launched the program, our participating colleges had waiting lists within the state. We could not accommodate all those who wanted to pursue the opportunity. That continues to this day, demonstrating the potential that always has been there. These young men simply need opportunity and guidance.

Not every young black male can sing, dance, and throw a ball, which is the stereotypical perception. Some want to be doctors, builders, or electricians. Some want to teach. Few people aspire to be what they cannot see every day. The young man who might have aspired to greatness might be left off the bus unless he is encouraged to make the most of his unique skills.

As we recruited Misters, we discovered youth who taught Sunday school, tutored their siblings, and served as camp leaders. They were teachers by nature, and we resolved to draw their tutorial talents out even more. We help the young men, who are interested in the program, understand how their experiences have shown that they are potential teachers.

We find recruits in every corner of South Carolina, and they find us. In our state, they have come from as far south as Beaufort County and as far north as Oconee County. They are young men who have the instincts to be good teachers—who harbored the passion for teaching in their hearts, but never before expressed it. They kept this passion, which cannot be easily measured, quiet; they did not want anybody to know. Why? Because they feared being ridiculed for wanting to pursue a "woman's job." People in the street culture would laugh at them, or worse. Such an attitude stands in stark contrast to the long tradition in which teachers, both women and men, were the pride of their communities.

Over the many years that Call Me MISTER has recruited teachers, we have sought to celebrate and re-instill that spirit. We created a recognized brand. We recreated that sense of pride in the profession. That, in turn, has further boosted recruitment. We get referrals all the time, from within our school systems, as well as from black barbers, like Mr. Brown, who will make a phone call to us, while a promising prospect is patiently seated in the barber's chair. Yet, we cannot possibly accept all the people, who want to be in the program. Even as we have grown from a network of four institutions to fifteen in the state, we still cannot handle everybody.

The pool of applicants has improved consistently over the years. We are not suggesting that they are better people, but simply explaining that they are able to do better on the standardized tests. They can easily get into college, and once there, they can thrive in the teaching major. The major is one of the toughest at all of our partner institutions, which require standardized exams (based on a national norm) to both enter the major and to become certified to teach on top of earning the degree. Call Me MISTER teachers must do what is required of their peers and profession. They receive no shortcuts because of race or background. Misters are challenged to raise the bar, not lower it.

Throughout this book, you will hear the Misters' stories in their own words. Nothing that we write here can exceed the power of these voices. We hope these voices will reach other young men who will see the potential in themselves and say, "That's like me." We hope that by reading about the Misters' experiences the policymakers, funders, and all other stakeholders will see the hope of what could be and say, "That's for us."

The Misters' stories tell it all. Young men, who have almost succumbed to tragedy or who have had trauma in their lives are buoyed to new heights—and Call Me MISTER has opened the doors to a great future in which they can give back in remarkable ways. In this book, it would have been impractical to capture the story of each and every Mister. The words shared here represent the spectrum of their journeys. These inspiring men are able to spread the seeds of hope.

IN THE WORDS OF THE MISTERS...

Michael Hopkins

"When I was growing up, there were a lot of us who were the same age, but a lot of people moved away. A lot of my classmates moved closer to Chester or closer to the city. There aren't any jobs in Blackstock, South Carolina—it's just a country town. For those of us who went to college, it was just like moving off.

"At the end of my freshman year, I had a black professor. He reached out to me and three other classmates and told us that Newberry College was trying to be a Call Me MISTER site and they wanted us to be the first class. I really wasn't sold. Quite honestly, I really didn't want to be an elementary school teacher. In order to become the first cohort, we had to participate in the first internship that summer. I went to the internship and learned a lot, and that's when I became sold. Being around all those guys and seeing their passion for MISTER—it was much bigger then myself.

"Most of the time, when you think about teachers, you don't think about African American males. I want to change people's minds, period, about African American males. Most people see African American males as rappers, drug dealers, [or] athletes. We can do a lot more than what we're seen as."

PART ONE

The Roots of a Crisis

CHAPTER 1

The Persistence of Stereotypes

The stereotypical image of black men comes right out of the days of slavery. The perception that they are shiftless, lazy, unaccountable, and irresponsible is perpetuated as young men internalize that message and come to view themselves that way. They see themselves as gang members and criminals. Going to jail becomes a badge of honor.

Gang culture, drugs, violence, and unprincipled sexual behavior—these are some of the contemporary manifestations of the old stereotypes. The perception is perpetuated by an abundance of data on educational underachievement, incorrigible school behavior, and opposition to authority. Call Me MISTER seeks to combat those images by going back to people's roots. The notion that black people are, by nature, deviants was never based on anything that resembled the truth. It was based on a desire to keep black people in servitude. It was all about control.

One thing must be made abundantly clear: History, in no way, substantiates those negative stereotypes about the black male. This stereotype was never who the black male was. That was not his story. Today's youth must realize that was not the story of their parents, grandparents, great-grandparents, or great-great-grandparents. Rather, it was a lie stemming from the slave-master and perpetuated to this day in film and television. If a lie is widely believed, it can become a de facto truth. Instead, such a lie must be exposed for what it is.

When the African was transported to the Americas from his native land, he did not come with an innate sense of servitude and inferiority. No scholarly reading of African history suggests that to be the case, nor do the accounts passed down by the elders. African Americans' ancestral stories do not match the common portrayals in history books.

A RICH, NOBLE HERITAGE

It makes a world of difference for a young black student to understand—to feel and believe—that he comes from a rich, noble background with pride and principles. It is uplifting for him to know his ancestors had a value system committed to family, community, religion, and culture, and that was dedicated to economic development.

Talking about what they learned of black history in school, many Misters have told us that their teachers taught them about little more than the "I have a dream" speech by the Rev. Dr. Martin Luther King, Jr. They say, they received rote information focusing on a few key people in history, who did not relate to South Carolina's story. It would seem the lessons of black history are not being delivered with any sort of depth of understanding. That is despite the state requirement, in effect since 1989, that every public school must include instruction in black history as a regular part of its curriculum. The goal of this requirement is "to ensure that the history of Africa and African Americans, their culture and experience, is integrated into the existing K-12 social studies curriculum."

Black history must go back further than the arrival of slaves on American shores. When you take that history back across the waves, you encounter great empires. You encounter tribal peoples with an ingrained sense of dignity that dates back thousands of years. In fact, notable scholars such as Ivan Van Sertima (*They Came Before Columbus*, 1975) have documented the African trade routes and the presence of Africans in the Americas long before the late arrival of Christopher Columbus. To this very day, few schoolchildren or college graduates are aware of even this fundamental fact of history.

The black man arriving on a slave ship was, in short, far from a blank slate—and yet that is how he is often portrayed in our schools' history texts. That is what our American narrative offers us, and seldom more. The narrative just provides numbers on slave ships; it does not begin with kings and queens, scientists, mathematicians, and dignified tribal culture. We learn little about that. Black men and women are not portrayed as rulers of their own people, owners of their own land, or controllers of their own economy and destiny.

During a trip to Africa, co-author Roy Jones experienced exchanging currency in a bank in Lagos, Nigeria. The bank was owned, operated, managed, and entirely controlled by black men and women, which was quite a contrast to a typical American experience in the banking industry. One can only imagine what the American child's belief and perception is about Africa and Africans to this day. It is doubtful they are perceived as owners of their own land and controllers of their own destiny.

If picking up the history and image of black people from the point at which they were made indentured servants and slaves, be mindful that such an approach changes whom they are perceived to be. Beginning with a people enslaved cuts off their long tradition of family and societal structure, denying them their ancestry. Though we elected a president with Kenyan lineage, few black Americans proudly identify with their African roots or country (presuming they know it). Most believe they hail from the fabricated "south side" of American cities. The genius of Dr. Henry Louis Gates may have pleased a number of celebrities as they explored their ancestral roots, but most black people were less than curious.

THE IMAGES STICK

Instead, the truth about a dignified ancestry has been set aside for the imaginings of television and Hollywood media makers. Consider how long it took for African Americans to even earn a presence on TV, and look at how they were immediately portrayed when they did: as poor, struggling, and undereducated individuals (as on *Good Times*), who were "scratchin' and surviving" and asking, "Ain't we lucky we got 'em?" There were no black people in sight in *The Andy Griffith Show*'s Mayberry—yet then they made up much of the population of most Southern towns, as they still do. You would think Mayberry was in Iowa.

The networks did not consider an accurate portrayal to be commercially viable. Think about how recent this experience was. Sure, it was just entertainment, and we all laughed and enjoyed it. However, this disparity exemplifies how the American narrative gets re-scripted. Though the facts become skewed, the images stick.

Even the epic saga of Alex Haley's *Roots*, broadcast in 1977, did little to counter Hollywood's current stereotypes about black people in America. The undignified portrayal of young black adults on TV "reality" shows would have our ancestors and elders turning in their graves. In the '60s, none of us would have imagined that the fight for freedom, justice, and equal opportunity would produce no better characters than those portrayed as on most of today's popular black reality television shows.

CLEAN, ORDERLY, AND STRUCTURED

The truth, however, is clear to many African Americans. They have heard the oral history that has been passed down for generations. This is a proud story. Their families did not feel impoverished. To suggest that these people had come from poverty would be insulting. Families separated their economic conditions from their value systems, and in that way they felt far from poor. Many of the Misters in our program come from those kinds of families and possess that foundational belief.

Today's families have inherited the attitude that one's dignity cannot be stripped away even if one's body might be enslaved. The slave owners could not succeed in their attempt to make human beings into blank slates. If you read the narratives of slaves, you will find that they might have acted one way in front of Master Jim, but as soon as he left they got on with the business of raising their families and educating their youth. Through ensuing generations, their family life remained clean, orderly, and structured.

Such is the true story of most African Americans. It is the foundation that has allowed them to grow, survive, and strive against all odds. Though they are portrayed as struggling, they know that through it all they have protected their families and nurtured their children. Even when money is tight and a mother raises her children in public housing, she tends to keep the apartment clean and make home-cooked meals. She disciplines the children. She is a dedicated parent raising her family in the type of neighborhood that many people dismiss as dangerous and riddled with drugs. She has held tight to pride. She may lack the sophistication and education to advance in a career, and she may need assistance, but she is in touch with the strong values that have been handed down to her.

You see this pride in communities throughout the South: In terms of money, families might fall into the poverty category. Yet, their homes are clean and orderly. They place doilies on the arms of the couches. The homes are humble and the furniture is dated, but they have pride in every corner.

By no means is it true that a child from a single-parent, low-income home is doomed to do poorly in school. Nor does economic stress mean that a home will be unkempt, undignified, or lacking in love, support, faith, and values. There are countless examples of families, who make homes full of abundant good qualities, while also facing economic struggles.

Unfortunately, over time these struggles take their toll on some families. In each generation, as people become more and more cut off from the upbringing that worked so well for so long, issues arise in the homes and on the streets. These issues can be deadly serious, and they must be addressed.

IN THE WORDS OF THE MISTERS...

Brandon McIntosh

"A lot of the Misters grew up working in lower-class conditions. When you hear the Mister stories, [the men] talk about having a single mother and [going to] poor schools, and then Call Me MISTER came into their li[ves] and they had their turnaround.

"My mother always instilled in me how important education was and to know that people were expecting great things from me. I was always involved in the church, always making good grades. I played in the marching and concert band—I played the saxophone.

"I remember when my mother would read *The Little Engine that Could*. I'll never forget that book. She always made me feel I could accomplish—that there is nothing that I can't do. You just put your mind to it.

"She worked first, second, and third eight-hour shifts. She made sure she attended baseball games, band competitions, [and] awards days. She understood that parental involvement was very important. She always made 'Greet the Teacher Day.'

"I knew I could always depend on my mom, even though my father was absent from time to time. He was in and out [in terms of] being a presence in my life. He would show his face from time to time, and then he would go MIA. At first, it used to bother me, but now I know it made me who I am: a great man. I achieved everything I wanted to because I had male role models in my life to show me the way. My grandfather and my uncles would give me advice. My grandfather went into the military in his younger days, and he worked as a chef in a hospital. He never talked about the wars because I believe it was traumatic. He never gave any details. He was always in church. He was a very humble man. He was full of wisdom.

"Grandmother was a mother figure. She worked in the home, [and was] a humble lady, always in the church and taking care of the family."

Marquice Clarke

"I only had one friend finish college with me. College is very expensive, [and it's hard] being away from Mom and Dad; some of my friends couldn't handle the financial burden. Some joined the military, and some found jobs.

"My experience with learning about MISTER was through my collaborator, Mr. Rudolph Wheeler. He's amazing! I'm going to try not to get emotional. Throughout my collegiate experience, it was very difficult, at times; it was rigorous. Like most college students, I wasn't ready for college, and there were times that I felt like the world was on top of me.

"There were times I felt like quitting. I was done with it, but Mr. Wheeler would give me a little bit more and a little bit more encouraging words. I'm 24 and Mr. Wheeler is 67, and I consider him one of my best friends.

"It may sound corny, but when I examined MISTER, and those five assessments, I thought, 'I've been doing this the whole time.' I didn't have all of it—I didn't understand all of it—but the servant leadership piece was something that I was familiar with.

"My high school did not prepare me for college. It absolutely did not prepare me for college. My guidance counselor encouraged me, but as far as academically, [the teachers] did not [prepare me]. But they did prepare me with leadership skills and socially. I was class president for three years, and I was nominated the class clown."

CHAPTER 2

The Drain of Social Problems

The statistics are staggering. In South Carolina, only slightly more than half of all students graduate from high school after twelve years of education—and among black males, only about four out of ten graduate on time. If you look at referrals for discipline, suspension rates, expulsion rates, and dropout rates, the African American male leads in all of those categories.

According to data from the South Carolina Department of Education, 6,265 students dropped out of school in the 2009-10 academic year. Of this larger number, 3,740 of the dropouts were males, and of these, 3,152 were non-white.

According to recent figures, 33 percent of black youths ages eighteen to twenty-four, who had high-school diplomas did not have jobs, and 10 percent of black youths ages fifteen to twenty-four were in jail (compared with 3.4 percent of Asians, 2.7 percent of Native Americans, and 5.2 percent of Hispanics).

Meanwhile, gangs have continued to attract black youth, and their influence is spreading dramatically from coast to coast. Although gang activity was once an issue of the North, East, and West, it has reached the South and is influencing youth as early as age twelve.

The negative statistics have continued to grow even during President Obama's administration, showing a rise in murder rates, gang activity, joblessness, incarceration, school dropouts, suspensions, and expulsions. The election of a president does not necessarily change state and local policies or laws. Schools are locally controlled, not federally controlled.

If a school imposes a zero-tolerance policy that puts a child on the brink of suspension or expulsion for bringing a plastic fork to class, that discipline is not a matter of who is in the White House. Schools can be federally influenced, with federal incentives, but they are controlled by locally elected officials; their funding comes primarily from property taxes, and hence from landowners.

The above means if an African American youth is dropping out or facing expulsion, the issue is something that is going on in the local community, not in Washington, D.C. Zero-tolerance policies, which often lead to school-based office referrals, suspensions, grade retention, and expulsions, have resulted in putting record numbers of black males in the juvenile justice system and in adult incarceration. Drs. Marian Wright Edelman and William "Bill" Cosby have called attention to this "school-to-prison" pipeline, while recent studies by such scholars as Drs. Ivory Toldson and John Lee have examined this trend and its policy implications in great detail.

The historical record shows a great deal of struggle as the descendants of Africans brought here against their will have established themselves indelibly as Americans. As we trace the evolution of racial relations, we can see the roots of today's social problems.

A MISSING SENSE OF PRIDE

Where do these depressing statistics originate? They come from perceptions instilled early in life. Children's perceptions of who they are shape how they feel about themselves, and they internalize those feelings. This internalization often gets worse as these young people age: Children who had never thought of themselves as failures may find themselves struggling and come to feel that, perhaps, they truly will not amount to anything.

The statistics come, too, from a lack of mentors and good role models for African American children, particularly young men. In South Carolina, a state whose population is 28 percent black, black males make up fewer than 1 percent of the elementary school teachers. The racial representation is far out of balance, and the state faces a daunting challenge in turning these statistics around.

Look at it this way: Out of the total number of elementary school teachers in the state, there are only about two hundred black males. There are over 600 elementary schools, so only a third of those, at most, could have a black male teacher. However, most of the black male teachers are concentrated in larger urban areas (such as Greenville, Columbia, Charleston, and Orangeburg), while others serve in rural communities. The reality is there are closer to 500 elementary schools, without a single black male teacher, and they have not had one in a long time.

We are trying to address this dire shortage. The majority of the primary-grade teachers are white and female. Though they may have good hearts and impeccable credentials, most of them simply lack the background, cultural empathy, and patience that will help them connect with their pupils in a way that truly advances learning.

What has been missing for young African Americans is a sense of pride and knowledge about their cultural history that stretches back long before the days of slavery. In the training for the Call Me MISTER program, we emphasize that history does not start with segregation or with slavery; instead, the roots of black history are in the soil of Africa.

Nonetheless, the experiences of African Americans since they forcibly were brought to these shores have led inexorably to conditions today. Though many black men continue to excel and thrive on strong family traditions, a disproportionate number exhibit undeniable personal traits—such as low aspirations, low self-esteem, and poor self-concepts—that lead to social problems.

AN ADHERENCE TO VALUES

Does the blight of poverty define the black experience in America? If you were to ask the vast majority of African Americans who grew up, technically, in poverty whether they felt those issues defined them, you would hear the refrain that such was not their experience. They consider their value system to be equivalent to that held by the middle class or the wealthy, even if others consider their economic conditions to be poor.

Such families do not instill the feeling that they are poor in their children. In fact, the idea of being poor does not occur to these children until they hear it from someone outside their community. To complicate the situation, we have the labels associated with welfare checks and housing projects. Such labels, which were rare before the 1960s, date to about the time of Lyndon Johnson's administration.

The great majority of African Americans believe in themselves, as did their forebears. They believe they can endure. They believe they can take on any challenge presented to them because they have overcome hardship and obstacles for generations. They believe in the betterment of themselves. They believe in education as a pathway to liberation and to a better life. No "welfare society" label is about to squelch that inner drive.

In that persistence, they have long turned to the solidarity of their communities. They have found their strength in what was tried and true for them, and they did not take refuge in alcohol or drugs.

THE PERILS OF DEPENDENCY

In today's youth culture, we are seeing that inner resolve breaking down, as young people lose their grip on the communities that long sustained and supported them. For generations, self-sufficiency defined black community culture in the South. People lived off the land. Even those who moved into town might still have been raising chickens or hogs. However, in the decades and generations that followed, as many migrated north and into cities, conditions and culture began to change, and people began regressing from self-sufficiency to dependency.

For decades, the African American communities have been losing their land grip in South Carolina. Each new generation would pack up and leave their piece of homeland behind. Land has an immeasurable impact on the ability of a family to sustain itself, and on the family's attitude and sense of roots. When people own land, they feel anchored: They become resourceful and dedicated to working things out for the long haul. This attitude is very different from that fostered by renting a city apartment. There has been no corresponding great migration of whites from the South, which is evidence in itself of what the black community has been experiencing.

That exodus of African Americans from the South is known as the Great Migration. From about 1910 until the Great Depression, about 1.5 million African Americans left for cities in the North and Midwest. After the Depression, movement slowed until World War II, when the migration resumed; another 1.5 million left their homes between 1940 and 1950. The movement continued at that pace over the next generation, as many African Americans moved to cities in the West, particularly in California. By 1970, about one of every seven black Southerners had headed to the North or West.

People who had been proud to be self-reliant providers found themselves in hard times, without employment and accepting provisions. For most, the assistance was temporary relief while they got back on their feet. The prevailing profile of a good American, however, is that of a contributor who works, pays taxes, and is involved in the community. Although that profile certainly describes the African American tradition of hard-working landowners, it did not seem to fit those who accepted the helping hand of government for any amount of time.

Welfare programs fueled the growth of these stereotypes. Government assistance comes in many forms—agricultural subsidies, for example, or bank and industry bailouts—but the programs designed to fight poverty and help the unemployed invariably invite more contempt than others. The insinuation is that those people must be lazy—they are not trying to work.

LIVING UP TO THE LABELS

The way people are labeled can become the way they see themselves, and the way they see themselves influences how they behave. They may cease to strive for goals. Those behaviors can become entrenched from one generation to the next. People who might have contributed greatly to society instead feel trapped in a system of disincentives that stifles innovation and self-sufficiency. As the poet Langston Hughes wrote: "What happens to a dream deferred?"

Each of us wants to be a contributor and to be productive. Nobody wants to come across as a leech on the system. However, frustration wears a soul down. Someone can lose faith that things will get better, thereby losing self-confidence and succumbing to negativity.

The above has happened disproportionately to black males who are perceived to be unproductive. Many no longer try to overcome their situations the way young people so often have done—by delivering papers, bagging groceries, picking up trash, or earning an honest dollar as best they can.

TROUBLE ON THE HOME FRONT

Besides the labels that weigh them down, some children are carrying something else—something inside them. In so many families, there are secrets that remain unspoken or that seem unspeakable. Abuse and molestation of women and children are prime examples. Anger festers; a child who harbors abuse-related resentment will be even more vulnerable in the social milieu that encourages broken lives. Social and family issues deepen the problems in the schools; in turn, problems in the schools deepen the family and social issues. The result is a mad downward spiral.

A young man's relationship with his father might be volatile—that is, if the father is even present in the home. Often, the young man is just getting more and more frustrated by living with his mother in a two-bedroom apartment, in which case no dad is allowed (if the housing is subsidized by the government, a mother cannot have a partner living with her). In many cases, this is a world of cinderblock walls and cold, concrete floors in a unit with dim lighting and no pictures on the walls. Imagine what daily life is like for the little boy coming home to that.

Other factors complicate the situation, such as the mother's values, whether she is unemployed or underemployed, and whether the home is a house or an apartment. In many South Carolina communities, apartment living is a relatively new phenomenon, and it has drastically changed the lives of black families. Many of us who grew up in South Carolina did not know anyone who lived in an apartment when we were children. It seemed everyone lived in a house and had a grandfather or grandmother living up the hill. Many have not seen this stability in our communities since.

As more and more people live in apartments, children grow up without a sense of ownership. When their parents do not own a house and land, the children face a new set of difficulties. A young man does not develop the skill sets related to home ownership, like mowing the grass, gardening, painting, carpentry, using tools, and the other things families do when they take pride in what is theirs.

In South Carolina, and across the nation, the problems are unmistakable. Young people are being challenged in so many ways. Students are dropping out of school. Young men, in particular, are being pushed out of school into disciplinary facilities. Many of them wind up in the juvenile justice system or back on the street with their peers, who are also troubled. If they are not watching television, playing video games, or possibly wreaking havoc in the streets, these young men are simply doing nothing, squandering their days in idleness. Such is the world of an alarming number of our youth.

DEFINING MANHOOD

For the children in those city apartments, worlds apart from living in homes and on the land, going outside means being exposed to street culture. If a family lacks cash, the temptations of street life beckon these children even more.

Where does a young man find the definition of manhood? He finds it by hanging out—at the playground at first, perhaps, until he can move farther. Other youth in the neighborhood wield a strong influence.

In time, he may find himself riding in a car with other youth, all of whom want money and none of whom have responsibilities, duties, or a sense of ownership. Not one of them seems to know anyone who does. This hanging out becomes a lifestyle, and that young man adopts an attitude that makes handling him exceedingly difficult for a teacher.

This young man may seldom see examples of responsible black men, either among the ranks of those teachers, or in his neighborhood. This was not always the case, as in this reminiscence by a South Carolinian, whose school days preceded desegregation: "When we were coming up, we saw the men in school," says Steward Lawrence. "We saw the strength…We saw the sign of power…We saw the neckties. When Mr. Code [the principal] walked by, we'd straighten up. He was the unspoken parent."

TEACHERS FROM ANOTHER WORLD

The challenge of teaching such young people is particularly tough for a white woman, who might as well be from another world. As she begins the school year, this young woman has perhaps just gotten back from a family vacation at the beach. She and her husband are homeowners, and he, too, has a college education. She has a close, extended family, and one of those relatives, or someone at church, encouraged her to become a teacher. Her world is stable. She and others like her make their way into the trenches of the underserved, who do not share her experiences.

In the classroom, the young man who lives in subsidized housing may look unkempt. He may not have had much sleep. The teacher sees him as sullen, disrespectful, or angry. She has no training to see what is really happening with him. Instead, dealing with this child seems impossible. She operates on a set of assumptions about kids from his kind of background.

It is not that children do not see African American teachers in the schools of many communities; rather, these teachers are very seldom men. Black women teach, particularly at the elementary level. However, a child who is dealing with a black mother or grandmother at home and with a black female teacher at school, does not separate the two. The way that the child views the mother is how he also views the teacher.

One of the baffling questions that we face is, why children in such situations still tend to perform at low levels—even without the race issue. Why would this be so? The teacher training is the same for teaching candidates regardless of race. The answer may lie in how a teacher views a child. Does the teacher see that ten-year-old as the next Barack Obama or as the next inmate? That attitude is hugely significant. It determines how a child will respond in class.

We make sure that the Misters in our program are acutely aware of that dynamic. How do they see such children in terms of ability to read and write? How do they feel about those children? The teacher's attitude is going to shape so much of what becomes of that child, who is looking for a role model and a mentor.

Few teachers have the ability to keep their feelings in check. When they think no one else is listening, they say things to one another about the children they teach. If those teachers develop a disdain for a culture they do not understand, they will engender that disdain among their charges, too.

In such an atmosphere, the child who "makes it"—getting Cs or even Bs, yet coming nowhere near his or her potential—is the compliant one who just sits quietly. The disruptive children, who are acting out require so much of teachers' and administrators' time, that the trouble-free ones simply get passed along. Little expectation and little development results in big damage.

THE EXAMPLE OF THE ELDERS

Young people would do well to heed the example of their elders, even if those elders are not their own relatives. If only the young could come to know those elders.

"I can live without money," an African American man in his nineties told us. We were interviewing him under an oak tree as the sun was waning. We were collecting narratives of black men for use in the Call Me MISTER program. He was still chopping wood, gardening, and growing his sweet potatoes. He was living without healthcare and without government assistance, and we knew the young men in our program could learn much from him.

The man meant what he said. He had never had luxuries or seen great achievements, but his voice was deep and flowed with energy. "I'm telling you, I've lived it," he said. He knew that the true measure of a man lies in persistence, principles, and productive work—and he did not need money to endure.

IN THE WORDS OF THE MISTERS...

Daniel Groves

"I've never had a black teacher. I never saw a person of my color in that position. Around fifth grade, I wondered why I hadn't seen a person of color as a teacher. In elementary school, you draw pictures of what you want to be, so one day I drew a picture of myself as a teacher.

"When I got to high school, I started digging into the history of African American teachers. I did this on my own. I started going online, and that's when I found out about Call Me MISTER.

"I never had the honor to experience a black teacher, and I really wish I would have. I had very little black history. When Black History Month came around, it was mostly lesson plans around the civil rights movement and Martin Luther King, Jr.—big leaders, Rosa Parks, and people like that. That's really all that I gained [in] African American history. I never knew anything else about black history, but I did learn from movies, which could also be biased [about] certain situations and events that happened. Honestly, my cousins and I, we never talked about it. I honestly feel bad and wish I could have done more. I wish I could have asked more questions about the heritage of black people.

"As a teacher, I will make sure my students know about their history. Sometimes it's not about just the kids of color—you have white kids who don't know where they come from. At the end of the day, I just want my kids to have an understanding of where they came from [and] who they are."

CHAPTER 3

The Evolution of the Issues

It is a mad cycle: Current social issues contribute to reinforcing old stereotypes. Old stereotypes contribute to worsening current social issues. The stifling of economic opportunity has long been a challenge—and a consequence.

Dropping out of school cuts young men off from so many options; even the military becomes off-limits. Many are unwilling to accept the menial jobs available to them—and in South Carolina, with the closing of the textile plants, even those jobs have dried up.

At the turn of the last century, the economy was agricultural and families were rural. Even little children were out working the land. Agriculture remained a large part of the rural community before World War II. When the textile mills arrived early in the twentieth century, the economy began to reflect a shift in how people earned their money.

For many, rural agricultural life slipped away; later, when those mill jobs had also slipped away, the workers could not shift back. The farms and the mills had sustained generations. People ran into trouble when the textile plants, the steel factories, and the military bases closed. The South Carolina economy has long been hurting.

Once African Americans began taking mill jobs, such jobs tended to stay in families. While working at the mills could be harsh and dangerous work, it did provide stability for communities. People met at the mills, and their families intermarried. Fathers, sons, uncles, and grandfathers all worked at the same mill. With such stability, family bonds can grow—not just within the nuclear family, but in the extended family as well.

Into the 1970s and 1980s, as those jobs continued to disappear, communities saw a profound shift. People left for jobs elsewhere, wherever those jobs might be. For those old enough to remember, the time could have seemed reminiscent of World War II, a time when a generation of men seemed to vanish from the labor force. Those men, who did not serve were not considered dating material by the women at home, many of whom, along with their children, assumed the jobs and worked the fields. Three or four decades later, communities became emptied of workers once again.

The displaced workers found jobs in the service industry. A large number of black workers served in homes, hotels, and restaurants, finding whatever menial labor they could for low wages. Some never worked again. For many, particularly those in rural communities, there was no next job. They waited for a paycheck that was not coming. No new industries were on the way. Some blamed community leaders for stifling growth.

One way or another, most people endured. Their innovation and resourcefulness brought them through tough times. Yet, the impact of the sagging economy has been profound. Moreover, it did nothing to dispel the longstanding image of the black man as someone who is unwilling to contribute.

THE IMPACT ON RELATIONSHIPS AND FAMILIES

When a young man finds himself unable to earn an income and unable to prosper, his attitude toward dating and marriage changes dramatically. If he has no money, it is easier for him to hang out with other young men, who are in similar positions. It is hard for him to have a girlfriend, since he cannot take her out. He lacks the resources to attract a young woman, losing out on the chance to fall in love and think of a future together.

This way, economic strife tears into the core of our humanity, defeating something as simple as young men and women being able to spend time together in a way that helps them develop their relationship into a cohesive family unit. Instead, men hang out together, and they do not seek courtship. A few decades ago, restaurant booths would be full of couples out on dates. Today, groups of young men arrive to sit at the bar. Young women, their babies in tow, come in with their mothers for a meal. Couples on dates are few in number.

Of course, there is not a lack of sexual behavior. Increasingly, children are born outside of thriving family units. The mother and father do not marry. Even if they were so inclined, their lack of money frustrates the goal; they have no jobs, no car, and no place to live. Starting a family seems beyond hope, and their lack of hope leads to problems in aspirations, attitudes, and behavior. If a young woman does manage to go to college, she is unlikely to return home and marry a man of such low status.

This is a pattern among poor people of any race, and in time it destroys people's self-esteem. How can a man see himself as a strong head of household, when he has observed two or three generations of fathers and grandfathers, who have been less than productive, skipping between menial jobs and unemployment?

Men and women alike see the pattern, and it hardly jibes with the history of self-determination that long characterized their forebears. They do not exactly feel like model citizens any more. In 1987, *Time* featured Asian Americans as the nation's model minority. What does such a declaration say to African Americans, Hispanics and other minorities? It tells them that they are not the models; instead, they are perceived in another kind of way. Those stereotypes attributed to them are, of course, no more desirable in their own communities than they are anywhere else.

Over the course of generations, the combination of this breakdown in economic structure and people's inability to earn an income considered worthy of family and community, contributes to the further breakdown of family structure and relationships. As pride and confidence deteriorate, so does a sense of responsibility and accountability.

As children grow, they watch the men and women around them. Society at large watches them, too, and stereotypes flourish. People begin to see youth, not as future leaders, but as thugs. The youth come to see themselves that way, too, and they behave accordingly. They lose hope for a productive future. Instead, their future becomes something to consider on a minute-to-minute basis.

Yet, hope does endure. People find their way, and their efforts must be encouraged. This encouragement starts in the schools. The history of education among African Americans has taken many turns—but through it all, their desire to excel has always been powerful.

A SKILLED LABOR SUPPLY

Since the 1600s, Southern slaveholders practiced capturing and enslaving human beings for purely economic reasons (developing a workforce to cultivate their rice and cotton plantations). Instead of enslaving the indigenous Americans, they drew instead on a highly skilled labor force in west Africa. The slave traders brought their captives to American shores in the holds of slave ships to support an economy that would make white Southerners, including those who owned the South Carolina rice plantations, very rich.

The elite population of white planters made up just a few percent of the population. Most whites, by far, were poor, although cultural historians have found that most of today's Southern whites typically believe that somewhere in the past, their families owned slaves. Statistically, that could not be true; yet these people's desire to identify with the planter class is a reflection of the long interplay of class and race that has shaped Southern history. Many whites have long identified with aristocracy politically and socially, and to this day, that tendency affects the psyche of Southern politics.

In the days of slavery, black people actually had more exposure to the highly educated planters than did the poor whites, who had no interaction with them. The slaves, by contrast, were able to observe how literate the planters were. When people witness literacy, they soon begin to want it for themselves. Even in the antebellum years, the African American community's desire for education was strong. It was there from the beginning, and it was passed on from one generation to the next.

A THIRST FOR EDUCATION

For decades, white Southerners—and South Carolinians specifically—strove to deny education to black children. Often, what people do not understood is that the black community—the ex-slaves, the freed men—wanted that education very much.

Looking back at the history of developing the universal school and the common school, we find clear historic evidence showing that the black community fought to obtain schooling for children right out of slavery. Literacy—simply being able to read and write—was desirable yet rare, and those who gained it were highly esteemed and influential. African Americans' work ethic was strong. People were industrious and determined to support their families.

The nineteenth-century white community, however, denied the black community anything that could uplift it. Yet, this community could not extinguish the flame. African Americans desired knowledge. They wanted schools, and both private and public ones developed. Even then, the property tax base supported public schools; yet, as blacks continued to seek out education and develop support for it, whites positioned themselves to take it away. It was a repeated pattern of give some, take it away; give some, take it away.

"Blacks emerged from slavery with a strong belief in the desirability of learning to read and write," James D. Anderson, professor of the history of education at the University of Illinois at Urbana-Champaign, wrote in his book *Ex-Slaves and the Rise of Universal Education in the New South, 1860-1880*. "The former slaves' fundamental beliefs in the value of literate culture were expressed most clearly in their efforts to secure schooling for themselves and their children."

Consider the following early commentaries on the importance that African Americans placed on education:

Harriet Beecher Stowe, *The Education of Freedmen*, 1879: "They rushed not to the grog-shop, but to the schoolroom. They cried for the spelling book as for bread, and pleaded for teachers as a necessity of life."

Booker T. Washington, *Up from Slavery*, 1900: "Few people who were not right in the midst of the scenes can form any exact idea of the intense desire which the people of my race showed for education. It was a whole race trying to go to school. Few were too young, and none too old, to make the attempt to learn."

W.E.B. Du Bois, *Black Reconstruction in America*, 1935: "The first great mass movement for public education at the expense of the state, in the South, came from Negroes…Public education for all at public expense was, in the South, a Negro idea."

William Channing Gannett, 1861 speech: "They have a natural praiseworthy pride in keeping their educational institutions in their own hands. There is jealousy of the superintendence of the white man in this matter. What they desire is assistance without control."

As these writings indicate, the ex-slaves were very much committed to education and the development of schooling for black children. Underlying the educational movement of ex-slaves, Anderson writes, were the values of self-help and self-determination. "This underlying force," he wrote, "represented the culmination of a process of social class formation and development that started decades before the Civil War."

THE ERA OF JIM CROW

The white population, by and large, was alarmed by this educational trend, and the nation saw early signs of the Jim Crow era's systematic discrimination and segregation: the rise of white citizen councils and the KKK, for instance, along with the imposition of voter validations. The aim of such discrimination was to disenfranchise the black Southern voters, who held the majority. The one-person, one-vote doctrine, after all, could lead to a host of black senators, congressmen, and governors.

In a serious blow to the abolitionist movement, the U.S. Supreme Court declared in the Dred Scott decision of 1857 that "the Negro has no rights which the white man is bound to respect." By the late 1800s, the doctrine of "separate but equal" had been established; the Supreme Court endorsed the principle in *Plessy v. Ferguson* in 1896.

THE CULTURAL DIVIDE

Well after the abolition of slavery, the relationship between blacks and whites continued to be based on a perception of inferiority and superiority. The divide, deeply engrained in our culture, has been carried forward through the generations. It has been part of the racial matrix in the Civil War, the Jim Crow era and segregation, the World Wars, and the civil rights movement, right up to the present.

Through it all, we have heard voices for equality. Early on, Frederick Douglas and others spoke out in the abolitionist movement. Yet, the Jim Crow era came nonetheless; the concept of equality was not the order of the day for white Southerners. For many, such equality was unthinkable. It would be generations, and many decades, before Southern blacks and whites could even be in a room together and have that conversation. Such has been the stereotype's power. It has destroyed not only relationships, but also people. Many have died as a result of the belief that all human beings are not created equal.

SIGNS OF HOPE

These stereotypes are perpetuated to this day. Barack Obama's election to the presidency was a milestone, but we have a long way to go. That America could put a black man in the White House twice, including Obama's re-election, is indeed a sign of progress, but this progress did not come close to ending racial and economic discrimination or the social divide.

There have long been other such signs of hope. At times, farmers have crossed the racial divide, with blacks and whites coming together to discuss issues of common concern. In the decades of Reconstruction immediately following the Civil War, America was positioned for racial cooperation. Thousands of African American slaves who were now "free" made up the majority of the population, and they wielded major influence in many Southern legislatures as elected officials. This was a time when the nation could have saved its soul, while it was emerging from the evils of slavery. Instead, the resurgence of white supremacy in the South would retard progress toward racial equality for the next fifty years.

EARLY IMPETUS FOR BLACK SCHOOLS

The post-Civil War development of public schools to support African American education involved deep social and political change. This change was further complicated by the fact that the black labor force was continuously slipping away to the Northern states. There was a significant movement out of the South, particularly of men. People felt a better education of black children could help stem that flow and retain the labor force.

Significantly, even during the worst days of oppression, blacks and whites developed positive relationships and supported each other.

The history of racial relations cannot be entirely viewed as that of two polarized cultures locked in mutual hatred. In partnership with African Americans, white philanthropic organizations, including the Anna T. Jeanes Foundation, the Julius Rosenwald Fund, the Phelps Stokes Fund, and the General Education Board, for example, contributed significantly to develop schools for black communities.

Early in the twentieth century, philanthropist Julius Rosenwald (president of Sears, Roebuck and Company) founded the Rosenwald Fund. With the Rosenwald Fund's support, more than 5,000 schools were built in fifteen states for the education of primarily rural African American children, whose segregated public schools in the South were woefully underfunded. This development took the form of a partnership: To receive a grant from the Rosenwald Fund, the mostly rural communities had to contribute matching public funds—and they did so, raising millions of dollars, as well as supplying labor and materials, so that their children might get a better education.

That education, however, was still a segregated one. People intended the infusion of money to keep white and black schoolchildren in separate facilities. Though the facilities for black children lacked resources, their teachers' dedication helped make up for it. "Segregation fostered a special sense of commitment among black teachers that helped to compensate for poor buildings, scanty equipment, and lack of books," Adam Fairclough wrote in *A Class of Their Own: Black Teachers in the Segregated South* (2007). "Many black schools owed their existence and growth to the vision and dedication of black teachers."

Many of these small Rosenwald schoolhouses, which had just one or two rooms, still stand today. After schools were integrated and consolidated in the 1960s and 1970s, the Rosenwald schoolhouses were shut down. In large part, these schools' success and sustainability directly resulted from local black labor—and the laborers' motivation was strong, considering the strength of the families' desire for their children to be educated.

Communities that had little money rallied to the cause, pitching in to get the work done with fervor and excitement. Notably, Rosenwald teamed up with Booker T. Washington, arguably the most prominent black educator of his day, to create the initial architectural design for the schools. Students attending Tuskegee University assisted them.

From 1907 to 1957, during this era of separate and unequal schools, a corps of black women known as the Jeanes teachers traveled throughout the South in support of rural black education. They did so as part of an initiative by the Anna T. Jeanes Foundation; their work, in particular, drew funds from a million-dollar bequest made by the Quaker philanthropist. These teachers, graduates of historically black colleges, sustained the teaching force for many black schools, including the Rosenwald schools. They played a significant part in developing a teaching force for the black community.

THE DECLINE OF AGRICULTURE

Anderson points out that the decline of agriculture played a major role in the development of schools, since black children rapidly withdrew from the agricultural labor force after 1910. That year, nearly half of black children ages ten to fifteen worked in agriculture. A decade later, the figure had decreased 21 percent, and it decreased again to 16 percent, when the Great Depression began.

"The migration of black laborers from the rural farm areas to the city was central to this emancipation of black children from daily labor," Anderson wrote in *The Education of Blacks in the South, 1860-*

1935. "The migration, which started in full force in 1914, was also a key factor in forcing the southern white agrarian classes to reconsider the idea of universal schooling for black children." In 1917, the U.S. Department of Labor looked into the migration issue and cited increased support for a system of black schools, to "keep the Negroes in the South and make them satisfied with their lot."

During the first third of the twentieth century, Southern black children finally had public elementary schools—long after such schools were universal for other children. After the Civil War, former slaves had waged a first crusade for state school systems, or common schools, in the South. When the planters returned to power in the 1870s, however, they thwarted the initiative for common schools, particularly for black children.

"Black southerners," Anderson wrote, "therefore had to wage a second crusade to establish common schools for their children." This crusade was the Rosenwald program of building schools, which began as laborers were migrating northward en masse. The efforts of both blacks and whites, along with Northern philanthropic causes, put a system of universal education in place by the mid-1930s.

A SEVERE TEACHER SHORTAGE

In 1900, according to a U.S. Commissioner of Education Report, there was one black teacher for every ninety-three black children of school age, while the white ratio was one teacher per fifty-seven pupils. The standard at the time was one teacher for every thirty pupils. To meet that standard while enrolling three-quarters of the black school-age population would have required an additional 53,373 teachers. This teacher shortage continued into the 1930s.

Black colleges and normal schools played a crucial role in the push for better schools. By the 1920s, these institutions had finally advanced to the point at which they could reasonably be considered as offering "higher" education beyond the elementary and secondary school levels.

"These institutions," Fairclough wrote, "trained an influential minority of black teachers and reached a far larger number of public school teachers—many of whom had never got beyond secondary or even elementary school—by providing annual summer schools. The presidents of black colleges were articulate advocates for black education."

Black colleges played an important role in supplying teachers to meet the shortage, which came as philanthropists, white school reformers, and black leaders struggled among themselves about how black children should be taught. "All groups understood," Anderson wrote, "that no system of beliefs could be transmitted to the millions of black schoolchildren except through the ideas and behaviors of black teachers." As a result, he wrote, "black teacher-training departments became battlefields of ideologies."

SETTING THE STAGE FOR INTEGRATION

Following Anderson's timeline, one could make a case for marking the period of a "third crusade" for "equalization" of black schools that began in the 1940s. The *Brown v. Board of Education* decision in 1954, ultimately declared that the very nature of segregated schools was inherently discriminatory, and thus a violation of the U.S. Constitution, opening the door to the era of civil rights and the push for integration.

Thus, people had already begun engaging the social forces that would eventually lead to integration and consolidation of public schools throughout the South. The migration to the North, in effect, shook the Southern white community into a change of heart about black universal education. The South wanted to keep its labor force. Even during the Great Depression, after the economy crashed in 1929, people were still building many of the Rosenwald schools. Black children were still going to school. By 1940, in fact, school enrollment of black children and white children had reached parity. Virtually the same percentage of each race was in school.

In *Brown v. Board of Education*, the Supreme Court ruled against segregation for the first time, but it did so only in regard to education, not other facilities. "Separate but equal" remained the law of the land in many regards beyond 1954, lasting until the Civil Rights Act a decade later. South Carolina schools, for the most part, remained segregated until 1963, although that does not mean they all integrated at the same time.

While the Supreme Court had ordered desegregation with all deliberate speed, nothing about it was speedy. Up through 1964 and the Civil Rights Act, through President Johnson's Great Society, and into the 1970s and the consolidation movement, white teachers refused to teach black children. Many people held the ingrained position that no matter what the government decided on the federal level, they would do everything in their power to keep the races separate.

Slowly, however, people integrated schools during this period, at the behest of the federal government. This integration also led to the consolidation of schools and the breakdown of black-controlled public schools.

The above, in brief, is the history of American racial relations' evolution since the era of slavery and the Civil War. The failures of Reconstruction led to the rise of domestic terrorism, the Jim Crow laws, and the "separate-but-equal" doctrine. Eventually, the government acted to reduce segregation in schools, and the South—and South Carolina, in particular—led the way in school desegregation cases.

THE LOSS OF A THRIVING BLACK CULTURE

Despite segregation, this period had been a thriving time for black culture. Black entrepreneurs set up successful businesses. Farm families sustained themselves off the land. Black people created cohesive communities in which everybody knew one another and held each another accountable. Each community protected its own.

That community behavior was largely lost after integration. The oppression of segregation had helped to instill among black people both self-reliance and the determination not only to survive but also to grow and develop. Schoolteachers, who recall that era, say their desire was not so much integration; instead, they wanted better equipment, books, and facilities so they could do their jobs as effectively as possible. They wanted their share of government funding, that somehow did not make it to their schools.

"It was not so much racial separateness that vexed black southerners as the principle of legal segregation, and the misallocation of resources that accompanied it," Fairclough wrote. "The primary aim of integration was to secure better schools, not to mix with whites.

"This produced a paradox. Blacks liked the sense of community and solidarity that segregated schools fostered. But they disliked segregation by law, on white terms, and the denial of equal opportunity."

Along with integration came a fight by the black community for the education of black children in black schools controlled by blacks. This was not, for many, a fight to become integrated with whites. Instead, it was a self-determined effort to establish black schools. People held the foregone conclusion that whites did not want blacks going to school with them, and blacks did not particularly desire their children to go to school with whites either.

Despite the inherent injustice of segregation, African Americans had no problems managing their schools and teaching their children. They wanted more support, but they did not necessarily want their children to go to white schools. Besides, it seemed unimaginable that white teachers would ever want to teach black children.

With integration and school consolidation, the dynamic changed, and entire communities began to lose those bonds that had made them creative and industrious. What was lost along with integration and consolidation clearly connects to today's issues and challenges faced by black communities. Facing those persistent challenges is the goal of Call Me MISTER, which is on the cutting edge of what may be considered a "fourth crusade" in advancing African American education through its mission to recruit and develop black male teachers.

By the 1970s, the consolidation of schools was well under way, resulting from the *Brown* case and the Civil Rights Act of 1964. Because of consolidation, schools had increasingly fewer black teachers. They lost black teachers, and they lost black leadership.

"The failure of integrated schools to live up to their promise has led to a belated recognition that many segregated black schools of the pre-*Brown* era had been successful institutions," Fairclough wrote. "A few were as academically successful as the best white schools."

What was the ultimate result of integration, consolidation, and the loss of black leadership and stability? By the turn of the millennium, schools had a severe shortage of black male teachers. African American education was suffering. This new phenomenon is not in keeping with African Americans' long history of craving education, even in rural and poor regions.

A NEW DIVISIVENESS

The era of integration has influenced black people's longstanding quest for education. Today's new scene presents difficult challenges. People who consider only the current landscape, without the historical backdrop, have a distorted perspective. It is crucial to understand the turn of events that led to this change.

Let us look at what has happened over the last fifty years since integration. African Americans in South Carolina's communities today feel more divided. People had believed and hoped that integration would lead to grand improvements. The black community has indeed melted in, but it has reacted to integration in ways that people did not predict.

In many pockets of the South, real signs of integration did not emerge until the early 1970s. Integration did not necessarily begin the day after the court cases were decided. It took a decade after *Brown* before the 1964 Civil Rights Act was signed.

In the early years of integration, and into the early 1980s, as black children and white children began going to school together, both races felt the same urge to excel. So much was happening, and everyone was affected. Many people went to college for the first time. Black or white, many felt that if they did not want to be stuck at the cotton mill or the farm, they needed to get out of Dodge. Technology and expectations were changing rapidly—and a lot of talented people left their communities. For those who remained, their lives would not be the same. It would be the old South no more.

INTERRACIAL DATING

By the 1990s, interracial dating had started becoming more common. This was significant because it required an adjustment for both black and white communities. Families had to react to this sociological development, this new face of integration. For the most part, the southern states did not have the cultural and ethnic diversity of the other states, particularly that of the Northeast. For generations, until the Hispanic population began to build, diversity was simply black and white. That is how many Southerners have come to see the world, even as people increasingly check "Other" when identifying their race on census forms.

Even today, people tend to feel uncomfortable talking about interracial dating. Integration is still happening. We are still in the thick of it. People put traditional values on the line, or even abandon them, and they are trying to grasp how they feel about that. As it became more common for black men to date white women, for example, how did black women feel? The dating ratio has been changing, and the shift is continuing. How did families of either race feel about this new type of freedom—this new America that seemingly was emerging?

THE LOSS OF A MISSION

In the Southern system of black schools, the teachers, principals, and other leaders had represented a mission and a vision. They were dedicated to the community's development, and black youth felt comfortable and safe. The teachers believed in their students, and the students knew it. The leaders enforced discipline. A code of conduct ran throughout the schools, homes, churches, and communities. These places seemed one and the same.

This collective mindset gave people a feeling of being united: People thought, "We are all going in the same direction, with the same vision and understanding of what it is all about." Back then, people say now, "We were all on the same mission."

With the coming of integration and the sharing of resources, not every school could continue to get support at the same levels. This was the impetus for consolidation of the schools. For the black community, consolidation meant elimination. It meant elimination, not only of schools, but also of personnel and of leadership. Such a loss came on the heels of decades of fighting for a better quality of education for black children.

"Ever since Reconstruction, black teachers had acted as community leaders, interracial diplomats, and builders of black institutions," Fairclough wrote. "Integration undermined those functions and diminished the relative status of black teachers. For some black teachers, integration brought demotion or dismissal."

The National Association for the Advancement of Colored People (NAACP) considered the loss of black schools "a price worth paying in order to secure a better education for all black children," according to Fairclough. The costs were indeed significant. Integration and consolidation had a huge impact on black children and white children—and, in particular, on the psychology of black males.

WHITE TEACHERS, BLACK PUPILS

With the onset of consolidation, black teachers were drummed out as many black schools were shut down. At this point, white teachers, who had been educated in segregated white colleges were teaching black kids, about whom they did not particularly care and about whom they knew little. These teachers were not interested in their black students' potential. Suddenly, white teachers were trying to teach black kids without even coming close to understanding them.

That is not to say there have not been many great, loving white teachers. Nonetheless, we lost an element of cultural sensitivity and nurturing. Black teachers came out of Allen, Claflin, Benedict, Morris, or Vorhees, all historically black private colleges, or South Carolina State University, a black public college. White teachers came from historically public and private all-white colleges in the state. Not one of the traditionally white colleges was doing much to prepare teachers to enhance the achievement of classrooms filled with black kids steeped in poverty.

Certification requirements were imposed, and teacher-training programs were revised. Many of the changes were good efforts, but the training became less culturally sensitive. All in all, the major shift during this period was from classrooms where black teachers taught black kids, to ones in which white teachers taught black kids. These white teachers adhered to standard practices that painted everybody with the same brush, whether the students were poor or wealthy, black or white, urban or rural.

By fitting people into the same categories and following the same models, the teachers aimed for the middle of the continuum of students. The children at the ends of that continuum fell outside the teaching zone, and teachers made little attempt to work with the students most in need. In such an atmosphere, parental involvement also suffered. Parents became less involved in how their children were faring, and they did not participate in making the decisions that determine a school's direction. Many students were left to negotiate issues on their own with a teacher or school officials. You can predict who wins in such a scenario.

Children who had been in schools that solely served the black community now found themselves in integrated schools with, perhaps, a 40-to-60 percent enrollment split between the races. Integration in enrollment did not necessarily mean the same, equal number of black and white kids with black and white teachers. That did not happen.

There is no example anywhere providing a majority group of black teachers instructing a majority group of white kids. You rarely even see a black principal at the helm of a predominantly white school. There are examples, but they are by far the exception. By contrast, many black schools have white principals and a majority of white teachers instruct large numbers of African Americans youth.

Consolidation did not mean the same thing for everybody. The ramifications were complex, and many other influences emerged, but the traditional black community was compromised. Many lost a sense of purpose and felt no connection with their community, no sense of identity there, and no celebration of black history. Black achievement levels fell, a direct result of who was in front of the classroom.

THE SCHOOL-TO-PRISON PIPELINE

Elected officials have long determined policy on how money is spent and for whom—and in educational history, it has not been uncommon for public funding to be diverted away from black schools in favor of white schools. Even today, in South Carolina, the fight over educational equity and funding continues.

Twenty years ago, 18 school superintendents sued the state of South Carolina. After twenty years, in which the case reached both a district court and the state Supreme Court, the case still remains unresolved. The affected districts tend to be poor black and poor white rural areas. The plaintiffs in the case claimed that the state formula for funding was inherently discriminatory against their school districts and failed to provide a minimally adequate education for the children they serve. The issues in this case, and today, are much the same as they were a century ago.

In contrast to school funding, consider the rate at which prisons are being built in South Carolina and in many regions. This rate is all tied in to dropout and literacy rates. Studies have found that fourth-grade reading levels correlate at high levels among inmates.

The path to prison starts in school. A child who is misbehaving tends to continue to do so. He is repeatedly referred out of the school system, a process that can start as early as in elementary school. By acting out in school, he winds up in a disciplinary school as a last resort and a last chance individual. When he continues to act out there, he winds up on the street, and when he continues to act out on the street, he winds up in jail. The child gets an increasingly detailed education about street life, which seals his fate.

This is the school-to-prison pipeline that we mentioned earlier. It is linked to zero-tolerance policies, retention, suspension and expulsions. It is a formula for disaster for troubled children. These are not the dropouts; they are the pushed-outs. Once held back, the child's prospects of ever completing school are greatly diminished. The child may never get what he needs to succeed, and failure becomes a foregone conclusion.

Children who are as young as twelve seem to be fearless about the prospect of incarceration. With the backing of his peers, the young man who comes to embrace prison life feels on top of his game. He gains in street confidence. So what if he spends two weeks, a month, or 3 months in jail? He will be coming back, with another tattoo, to the applause of his peers.

That young man also will have little chance of returning to school, thereby achieving much less employment. There will be no future for him on Main Street. He will be damaged and possibly dangerous. Feeling marginalized and disenfranchised, he will have no qualms about taking things that he believes he was denied. The system was not in his corner to begin with, he will believe, so why should he care? Why should he care about teachers, schools, authorities, or anybody?

What does he need? He needs a new image, a new vision for himself, and a better sense of direction. He needs an agent of change: a mentor with principles, understanding, and a sense of ownership. He needs someone to look up to besides a rapper who celebrates gangsta culture. He needs someone, who communicates that a person should dread going to prison for senseless crimes, not be proud of it. The ones who can be proud are those who paved the way: the black youth who went to jail for the cause of freedom, justice, and the right to equal educational opportunities.

A young man in trouble needs someone who cares—someone like a Mister.

IN THE WORDS OF THE MISTERS...

Kwadjo Campbell

"I have had a blessed journey along my path to becoming a Mister and an educator of children. Who I am today reflects the family, community, and neighbors I grew up with while attending school and in the workforce. There are always a few who stand out in memory—people who inspired, pushed, or gave you valuable lessons. I was blessed to have Dorothy and Dorothy in my life. Dorothy Gale gave me a fierce model of womanhood. She was my grandmother, and she was bold, reverent, and a matriarch in every sense of the word. She bowed to no one, except my granddad. Dorothy Wright was my twelfth-grade AP English teacher. She told me that I was special—that I had a special gift to give to the world—and I believed. I was also blessed to have L.J., Fred, Dr. D., Uncle D., Doc Jones, Big Daddy, and my granddad in my life as well. These men have given me a model of manhood: self-determined, selfless, academic, courageous, grounded, and humble. These models of womanhood and manhood have guided me along my journey.

"I come from the Eastside of Charleston, South Carolina. It is an urban Southern community rich with history and tradition, including the first AME church in the South, Emanuel; Fisherman's Wharf; Gullah culture; and the Philip Simmons Blacksmith Forge. It is also a haven for poverty and crime. Unfortunately, I was not able to escape unscathed as I had numerous brushes with the law. Even when I went to college and became a local professional, it was hard to cut ties with certain elements of my past. I call it the 'Michael Vick dilemma.' I entertained the foolish talk of childhood friends instead of 'bringing them up.' This is a lesson I pass on to younger Misters who enter a very public field as a teacher. I believe in staying rooted to where you come from, but I also believe we have a duty to improve the community by bringing others up morally, economically, and socially.

"I always wanted to be a teacher, and I would have been one straight out of college if it had not been for my false sense of urgency as it relates to the dire conditions in the African American community. It's not that the issues aren't in urgent need of addressing—I am speaking of my perception that I had to solve our problems today. Another lesson I can pass on: Real solutions take time to build, and change, for the most part, is gradual.

"After leaving politics, and [after] a stint as a manager in retail, I pursued admission into Dr. Lienne Medford's program at Clemson—she [directs] Clemson's Master's of Art in Teaching Program—and was accepted. She informed me about the Call Me MISTER program and encouraged me to get in touch with Mr. Winston Holton and Dr. Roy Jones.

"'Who?' I asked concerning the last name.

"'Dr. Roy Jones. He is the director of the program.'

"I knew Dr. Jones. He was a mentor of mine while I was a student at the College of Charleston. He got me involved with mentoring while I was a student there. I was [a mentor] at Courtney Middle School, as a matter of fact. Life has a way of coming full circle, or at least running in patterns. The rest is history, as they say.

"The journey has been a tumultuous one. The MAT program itself was tasking, but I managed to come through with a 4.0. I currently have a 3.9 because of two courses I took within the Upstate Writing Program here at Clemson with Dr. [Rebecca] Kaminski. I feel more than ready to help my students succeed in the classroom and life. The Call Me MISTER program has also been critical in my success. This program made it financially feasible for me to fulfill a dream, switch careers, and impact lives in a way I never could as a retail manager.

"The program has also helped me feel like I am part of something bigger than myself and helped reinforce the idea that I am here for a purpose, not just a job. Today's schools need to be armed with teachers who understand this. We are here on a mission.

"My journey to graduation and the classroom has taken longer than I expected. I was supposed to be done in one year—Clemson's MAT Program is accelerated. That was the plan my wife and I mapped out as we financially prepared for my career switch. My earlier brush with the law came back to haunt me, as I was denied approval from the Board of Education to student-teach. Heartbroken, but not defeated, I began a new leg on my journey. It took two years, but finally, after receiving a pardon from the State of South Carolina, I was approved by the Department of Education! Along the way, I was able to take additional courses that have given me the opportunity to be[come] dual-certified. So, while I tarried for my approval, I stayed in the education sector by taking classes and working in the classroom. It has been a blessing. As my writing professor Dr. Kaminski reports, I have grown as a teacher.

"My journey has been a blessed one with great role models, a strong support system, and obstacles that have only served to make me a stronger human being and more prepared teacher. I want to be for my students what my role models were for me. I want to be the inspirational teacher they write about thirty years from now. I want to teach in communities in need of light because only light can drive out darkness.

"I want to teach in a school that allows me to use my other talents—ones garnered from my previous career—so that we can bring in additional resources, build additional programs, and impact the community in a way that goes beyond purely educational benefits. I want to give back all that has been given me, and then some. I am grateful for the people and experiences that have made me the Mister I am today."

PART TWO

Opportunity for New Growth

CHAPTER 1

The Mission of Call Me MISTER

We believe that Call Me MISTER is indeed in the vanguard of a fourth crusade to ensure a quality education for Southern black children, building upon the advances of earlier generations.

Educators and other scholars concur that the best way to improve student achievement is to place highly effective teachers in the classroom. As districts struggle to find those teachers, the children living in extreme poverty—rural and urban, black and white—suffer the most, particularly the youngest pupils.

Our goal is to find and develop those native-born souls who will be committed, first, to raising the bar for their own education and then to reaching back to lift up and empower others. In the process of achieving this goal, Call Me MISTER has released a magnetic and transformative human synergy.

A HOMEGROWN APPROACH

From the onset, we intended Call Me MISTER to be a homegrown approach to recruiting, developing, and placing teachers. We intentionally targeted it for African American males. Our expectation was not global or national in scope; rather, it focused on the shortage of black male teachers, especially at the elementary-school level, in South Carolina. We believed we could draw a pool of students from the state who would stay in the state and teach in a public school.

At the elementary-school level, teachers have been predominantly women. For some, the perception has become that teaching is a woman's job. Some people also perceive that black males only pursue college for the sports programs, other majors, and extra-curricular activities. They believe black males are not inclined toward the talents and virtues that lend themselves to a teaching career.

On the contrary, a significant number of children and teens are not necessarily good at throwing a ball and simply do not keep in touch with the broader entertainment world, but the thought of teaching is appealing to them. They also tend to be family-oriented and are at home in the evenings, often helping to watch out for younger brothers and sisters and nurturing those siblings. These individuals experience responsibility and hold themselves accountable. Unknowingly, they already are acquiring some of the dispositions and skills that all good teachers must possess.

The lure of other careers has also reduced the pool of male teachers. During the days of segregation, many vocations were virtually closed off to African Americans. They could not aspire to the training and education needed for those professions. Later, as opportunities opened up, young people began to shift away from the professions of teaching and preaching to look at options like business, medical, engineering, and law schools. These and other professional careers beckoned to the best and the brightest, leaving a smaller pool of students to pursue teaching.

Meanwhile, an onslaught of social issues, including drug abuse and violence, took its toll on others, who might have been prospective teachers. As high schools' dropout rates swelled, many good young minds lost out on a promising future.

Call Me MISTER is working to turn that around at a grassroots level. The program has demonstrated that young people can be excited about becoming teachers. The profession teaches by both books and example. In seeing a role model and a strong black man in front of their classroom, children also see possibilities for themselves.

TEACHING AS A TRUE CALLING

We raise teaching to the level of a calling. Teachers have an impact that lasts for generations, and that impact transforms communities. The program helps the Misters understand that calling. It develops them for that role. The Misters get more than a degree and certification. They get true qualifications: they get the ability to build communities and change the educational environment.

The program helps young black men to step up in a way that society has not seen often enough in a long time. Participating in the program is about far more than getting a job with benefits. Participation is about serving, leading, and loving. It is a given that African American children need qualified, effective teachers. Yet, they also need teachers whom they can imagine themselves growing up to be like. They need positive role models and mentors: strong, healthy, and committed men and women.

The Misters serve as a profound example for both black children and children of all races. It is essential to plant appropriate images of racial relationships in young minds from earliest childhood. All children need to see examples of good men taking charge and showing leadership. This helps fight stereotyping and racism. When a white child comes to look up to a black man and aspire to be like him, this development of respect works wonders toward fighting the hatred that has permeated racial relationships for so long. It changes what becomes implanted in the heart.

To respect a teacher is to honor his or her position of authority. Teachers have long commanded the respect, not only of pupils but also of the public. Unfortunately, that respect has been eroding. They are losing the esteem of their students and of greater communities.

Call Me MISTER aims to rekindle the spirit of respect for teachers and education that was the norm in African American culture for so long. The program helps young people, pupils as well as teachers, reconnect with their cultural heritage so they can understand their legacy and the value of instilling it in the next generation.

DEVELOPING SERVANT LEADERS

We strongly believe that the formal education of undergraduate and graduate students simply does not go far enough, particularly in preparing teachers for the pupils located in the many different communities that we aim to reach. We have developed a philosophy regarding what will transform the young men who come into our program into highly effective and competent teachers—in other words, into Misters.

The program does not seek shortcuts to teacher certification, nor does it attempt to circumvent the current requirements for becoming a teacher. Young black men today must be confident that their credentials and competency are above reproach. They cannot slip into the profession through a side door. Nothing must compromise the gains made in the long struggle for black education in the South.

African Americans must never forget the history of their journey. Overcoming obstacles is nothing new in the black experience. The

Call Me MISTER challenge is to build capacity and empowerment in black males, so that they can take on any hurdle that may come their way. The program's work begins with meeting the demands of the teacher education and certification program.

We must make the important distinction that Call Me MISTER is not the teacher education program. It is housed in the participating colleges' education departments, but it is a non-secular oriented, servant leadership development program. It is delivered separately and concurrently from the traditional training, as a co-curriculum.

The co-curriculum's regular weekly meetings, summits, internships, mentoring, community engagement, and service efforts all are aimed at developing the young men's mindset, attitude, outlook, and disposition. The activities are designed to help them understand the value of their journey. That perspective is critical in producing the kind of teacher, who is committed to community and family, and to develop a teacher who will focus on the educational issues of the least-served.

You have to "reach them to teach them," says Atlanta-based education specialist Hotep. The extent to which a teacher can connect with the hearts of pupils and understand their backgrounds is the extent to which that teacher will inspire achievement. This inspiration requires a personal teacher-student relationship. To produce such a teacher and such a leader takes a special kind of development, one that is lacking in the formal curriculum.

That is where our co-curriculum comes in. We concentrate on multiple dispositions. We look at how the Misters view themselves, and we evaluate their sense of service. Teaching must be service-oriented, since there are so many other ways to make more money. A good teacher needs the heart of a servant leader. Through self-assessment and interaction with their peers, the Misters become better prepared to address the challenges confronting those students often marginalized by academic failure.

As we work on the Misters' dispositions, we also develop their professional acumen. They come to see how attitudes influence a teacher's classroom performance. We want the Misters to understand the kind of personal profile that will allow them to stand before a classroom, be respected, and impart respect. Dr. Lamont Flowers, executive director of Clemson's Charles H. Houston Center for the Study of the Black Experience in Higher Education, has conducted assessments on the Misters' dispositional development. Dr. Flowers' findings support the significance of these personal attributes.

A "LIVING LEARNING COMMUNITY"

Many of the Misters come by these social skills naturally and have learned them through interactions in their homes and communities. We strive to make sure they develop the essential traits for success. As part of that effort, we encourage their interaction as members of cohorts in our "living learning community."

We believe that the Misters' experience in small cohort groups is crucial to their success. It is hard for peers to fool one another. They live together; they go to class together. They see each other in their best moments and their worst moments, and they get regular feedback from the entire group. That allows each to test his own growth against the cohort's. That is how we assess their progress, too. They evaluate themselves; they evaluate one another; and we, in turn, evaluate them. The process continues through their college years, as we develop them to subsequently become professional teachers as servant leaders.

Meanwhile, the Misters go through the same formal education and preparation required of any teacher. They must meet all of the institution's graduation requirements, although we believe their enhanced training and sense of mission makes the profound difference between them and most other pre-service teachers.

The Misters come to their own decision about whether teaching is the best choice for them. They face exams and standardized tests to get into the major, to graduate, and to become certified to teach. This is a commitment they cannot take lightly, and it is best that they understand quickly what it will mean to teach kindergarten, third grade, or seventh grade.

PREPARING FOR THE CHALLENGE AHEAD

As in so many professions, the field of education can have a club culture. We want Misters to understand that they will often stand apart from the culture of the profession and the schools. An elementary school's community of thirty-five teachers, mostly women, who have been working together for some time, will develop an affinity for one another and a way of working and doing things. Teaching assures them of a comfort level: They are off work at 3 o'clock and home with their own kids. This is a secure job with benefits and summer breaks. It provides insurance for the self-employed husband.

Such a culture will draw to itself the same kind of personalities. Teaching can become more about achieving a lifestyle than about the mission of changing lives. New hires will tend to be those who seem to fit in with that lifestyle. True, the hiring process has checks and balances, but when all the professionals who are responsible for hiring have a similar background, and the pool of applicants is large, the results are not hard to predict.

That is why a blue-ribbon school can still have 10 to 15 percent of its student body not doing well. That 10 to 15 percent is the same population that is not doing well at schools without such acclaim. How does one account for that similarity? In both cases, the faculty members have the same backgrounds and the same preparation from the same institutions, and they have the same orientations. They are led by administrators, principals, and superintendents who come from the same system. What do you get? The same old story.

When a Mister enters that environment, he can tend to have difficulty because he is, in effect, counter to the culture by nature and by nurture. We cannot deny issues of class, race, and socioeconomics. In some cases, the race, class and culture appear the same, but still unwelcoming to the newly hired Mister. We want the Misters to be prepared for that and to be encouraged that they will make a mark. When a Mister leaves us, he enters an entirely different assessment and evaluation system. From that point forward, the schools will judge him. The very culture from which the Mister might have felt himself standing apart will be weighing his effectiveness as a teacher. Such a circumstance can be very unforgiving.

Come what may, these young men stand ready. They tell us regularly that the mission sold them on the program. They felt part of something bigger than themselves. Young people are eager to accept a calling. Call Me MISTER makes the most of their hunger and desire to make a commitment.

IN THE WORDS OF THE MISTERS...

Keith Wilkes

"The first day my mom took us to the all-white school—my brother, my sister, and myself—it was as if we [had] stepped off the moon. I remember the playground, dodgeball and everything else. All the kids were playing, and when we pulled up in the car and got out and began walking, all the activity stopped. The kids, the adults, just stopped and stared as we walked in. My mom acted as if she were totally oblivious to anyone staring, as if she were Rosa Parks. She didn't seem to let it bother her at all. She just looked straight ahead and carried us into the school.

"My time in a segregated school is what made me who I am because my integrated time was so nasty. Going to an all-black school was like *Cheers*; everybody knew each other. Teachers knew your parents. It was the whole atmosphere. Everybody was black: teachers, principals, custodians, cooks. Even when we walked to school, the elderly blacks were sitting on their porches in the morning and waiting for you on their porch in the afternoon. And they'd say, 'What did you learn today, boy? You make sure you get your lesson today.'

"My mom would tell me, 'You realize that Mr. So-and-So and Mrs. So-and-So, they can't read or write, and they're learning through you.' When we grew up in segregation, we were always told there was a better life. We were encouraged. I was always encouraged by other [black] people that there was a better life.

"I hope that I'm showing a kid—it's hard for me to put into words—that black men are just like anyone else, that we have the same hopes, we have the same dreams, we share the same goals, [and] we are all equal.

"I tell my students that a lot of my teaching is not [from the] textbook; it's life lessons. I have kids that come to me and just want to talk. Toward the end of class, I would ask my kids, 'Are there any questions? It doesn't even have to deal with what we did in class. Just any questions whatsoever.' And, some of the questions I would get, I would answer honestly and truthfully. And then after class some of them would hang back, and as they walked out they would say, 'Thank you, Mr. Wilkes.' And I would say, 'For what?' and they would say, 'For answering my question...I never could get anyone to answer that question.'

"Kids learn as much *for* a teacher as *from* a teacher, and I truly believe that. If they [the kids] don't believe they can make that connection, some of them won't open up to you. I feel as though I am their teacher, their nurse, sometimes their social worker, their psychiatrist; it's the whole gamut. A lot of people think teaching is you giving information and your day is done. No, it's not! There is a lot more involved than that, and a lot of people don't realize that.

"I didn't even buy a yearbook when I went to school. Now kids come back and ask me to please sign their yearbook. I am probably no different than any other teacher, but I'll see 'Please do not write on this page: Mr. Wilkes only'—and I'll take the time to write on there.

"I tell them the only thing we have different about us is our skin color. I say we all have a heart, two lungs, and two kidneys—and a lot of the kids, they take that to heart. And I say: 'I really, really hope that I get that across to you, that I care about you, and it doesn't make a difference what color you are.' I really think some of them get that. I hope that I am an everyday person do[ing] what all teachers do.

"Come Black History Month around there, I'm the only one that puts anything up on the bulletin board. My black kids don't even want to do it. My white kids or my Hispanic kids will do it. They [the black kids] do not want to call attention to themselves—even the biracial kids don't want to acknowledge the black side of them[selves].

"I [tell] my kids, 'I don't care if you are black, white, or fudge ripple.' They get a kick out of that. What shocked me this year—out of the few black kids or biracial kids I had, one of the biracial kids went back and told a teacher and started telling parents that I'm harder on the black kids then I am on the white kids. One teacher came up and told me that so-and-so said you are harder on the black kids. That really shocked me and it hurt me. I said, 'You've got to be kidding!' So, I got all my black kids together and I said, 'You guys think I'm hard on you, and yes, I am hard on you—it's because I expect a lot out of you. If I did not expect anything out of you, and I let you just sit there, then I [wouldn't] need to be in this classroom.' I said that if there is any teacher that does not expect a lot of you, then they're not doing you justice. And that should be the way it is all through your life. People should expect a lot out of you. And, after that, I pretty much saw a change in some of them. And they tried harder and seemed like they responded better.

"We had, I think the final count, sixty-seven teachers on the entire faculty at my [middle] school. I'm the only black male on the entire faculty at my school. We lost three males this year. We have six males on the entire faculty; everyone else is female. The ladies I work with—they are fantastic. I really mean that; they are fantastic. They are a professional group of ladies, and I see the dedication from my group… and how they care about the students. That's why I love working with them. I am no superman, but when they have a problem with black kids, they will come to me and they will ask me, 'Will you talk to them?' They just don't write them [the students] off. And I'll try to talk to them.

I love the team I'm on, and I love the ladies that I work with, and I wouldn't change it for anything."

===

CHAPTER 2

The Early Days

We held the first conversations about developing the program that would become Call Me MISTER in the late 1990s, when those with a vision for the initiative began meeting to share ideas. The people involved included educators, elected officials, civic and business leaders, superintendents, and principals—and, of course, the financiers who were trying to pull together sources of support. We knew it was a great concept, but it was going to take money, and getting it off the ground took several years.

Clemson University, a state institution, first partnered with the private colleges Benedict, Claflin, and Morris, with clear objectives for each. The colleges had a history of success in developing black teachers. Recruitment, development work, and placement would take place at those colleges. Clemson's role in the collaboration was to do the background research, data collection, marketing, and fundraising to support the effort.

The program was collaborative from its inception, with a focus on South Carolina's need to address the shortage of black male teachers, particularly in public elementary schools. That is how we initially defined the program's mission: to recruit, retain, certify, and place black male teachers.

Though Call Me MISTER is based at Clemson and originated there, we launched it through an agreement among the presidents of all the partner colleges. Clemson never felt it could manage the program alone, although the university provides full-time staff support and office space that serves as the program's headquarters. For well over a decade, the partner colleges' presidents—James Barker, Luns Richardson, David Swinton, and Henry Tisdale—have held steadfast in a biracial commitment to educating a new generation of African American male teachers to serve the state.

We consider the program's true beginning as taking place in the fall of 2000, when it launched. We recruited the first students from the high school senior classes that had graduated in the corresponding spring. In the ensuing three years, the program recruited classes and raised money from foundations, private sources, and individuals. Unfortunately, by 2003, that money had begun to run out. If there were to be a class of 2004 and beyond, we knew the program would need additional commitment and funding. (As an incentive for its students, the program provides partial tuition assistance and loan forgiveness options.)

At this critical point, we expanded the program beyond historically black colleges, to include historically white colleges and universities, along with a select number of two-year technical colleges. By the fall of 2004, recruits were coming to Clemson.

BROADENING THE SCOPE

As a direct result of that expansion, the appeal of the program, whose reputation was already established, increased. At a major conference in 2005, we determined that other states besides South Carolina were grappling with the same problem of the shortage of African American male teachers and the enormous educational challenges confronting black children. We heard the same questions from hundreds of people from 13 states: What had we done? How did we do it? Did we have plans to expand the program in other states?

The program was receiving national recognition. Even before the national conference, Call Me MISTER and Jeff Davis had been featured on *The Oprah Winfrey Show,* and received funding from Oprah's Angel Network. *USA Today* and other media outlets published feature articles on the program. Major organizations also became interested and began to promote Call Me MISTER. By 2007, we were receiving extensive positive publicity, which was quite beneficial in boosting the program.

Our documentary about early graduates, produced that same year, gave the Call Me MISTER program tremendous exposure via broadcasts on South Carolina Educational Television. By that time, a growing number of Misters had completed the four-year program and had gone out in the teaching force, so our documentary was able to both follow their progress and observe those recruits still in training.

The documentary focused on storytelling and on describing the Misters' own journeys. In it, we took a hard look at the issues, how they had developed, and how both the program and the young men, whom it launched as teachers were striving to resolve them. The documentary dove to the very roots of the Misters' world—families, communities, and schools—in South Carolina. It examined the heritage and legacy of these young African American men and the unique program that helped them tap the potential that might otherwise have remained hidden.

MORE EDUCATION, LESS INCARCERATION

All of those involved in developing the program agreed that people needed it and that its mission was important. Some, however, had serious doubts about the prospects of getting black males emerging from high school to consider teaching in elementary or mid-level schools. What evidence, they asked, showed that black youth had any such inclination?

True, many of the young black men, who might have been able to pursue college degrees, were being lost in the pipeline. Those who did go to college chose other majors besides education in a distinct shift away from the foundation upon which the historic black institutions were built. These colleges, after all, were set up as training grounds for developing future teachers and preachers.

Because the tradition of valuing education has not been passed on to many of today's black youth, they have not considered that teaching could be an honorable profession for young black men. Frequently, in recent generations, black children have gone from kindergarten through high school, without ever having had a single black male teacher. If they do, the teacher is usually a high-school coach who teaches social studies or physical education.

How likely was it, then, that a black male just out of high school would regard teaching at an elementary school as a manly profession? Because of these perceptions, political and educational leaders needed to be persuaded that Call Me MISTER stood a chance of success.

In the end, we persuaded them with this: They knew what it cost to build prisons. They knew that black men made up 65 percent of the state's prison population. They knew the costs of crime. They realized that the state's need for prisons directly resulted from a population in need of a better education. Why not begin to counteract the trend by improving the quality of the teaching force with black men?

Perhaps, they reasoned, if they spent more money on education, they would need less for incarceration. The idea clicked.

IN THE WORDS OF THE MISTERS...

Thomas Cayruth

"The internship with MISTER gives you a lot of experience with teaching. During the duration of the summer, you are teaching. Just having the opportunity to deal with children, you start learning who you are. You can say that you want to teach, but it's not exactly how you think it is going to be.

"My life wasn't necessarily rough, but I can relate to children who go through things. I use to have some behavioral issues when I was younger. So, it's easier for me to deal with children who have those issues. I feel like I can help them out more because I've been there. [Regarding] children who have behavioral issues, I guess I am especially sensitive to it because it's not always their fault. A child that comes to school that is not happy, [you know] there is a reason for it. There is a lot that has to do with the home life and family issues.

"I had no black teachers [in elementary school]–my only male teacher was a fourth-grade science teacher. He was a white teacher. I had one black male teacher, Mr. Johnson, in middle school; the rest were female teachers–no change in high school."

CHAPTER 3

How the Program Works

The Call Me MISTER program combines the special strengths and resources of Clemson University with the individualized instructional programs offered by Benedict, Claflin, Morris, and South Carolina State. In addition to these historically black institutions, the program has partnered with six historically white colleges: Anderson University, Coastal Carolina University, the University of South Carolina—Beaufort, the College of Charleston, Southern Wesleyan University, and Newberry College. In addition, the program has also partnered with four technical colleges: Greenville, Midlands, Tri-County, and Trident. To provide them with even greater opportunity and access, we give students the option of first attending one of the two-year partner colleges, before transferring to one of the four-year institutions to complete the baccalaureate degree.

To become eligible for Call Me MISTER, a candidate first has to submit an application for admission into one or more of those institutions—which, at the time of this writing, total fifteen. (See the Call Me MISTER website for details: www.callmemister.clemson.edu.)

Before we are able to consider them for selection in Call Me MISTER, the applicants have to be accepted into at least one partner college. The program is not a doorway into the partner college; instead, the partner college is a doorway into the program. The very first step, then, is for a prospective Mister to follow standard admission and financial aid procedures for applying to our partner institutions; the next step is to verify that they have been accepted. They also have to submit evidence they qualify for financial aid, if it applies to them. Qualifying for financial aid is not a requirement for participation in Call Me MISTER, unless the applicant needs to receive tuition assistance or any other form of financial support offered by the program.

Beyond these requirements, we take the candidates through another level of screening in which we ask them for additional essays. We interview them, both individually and in groups. We encourage a campus visit, if it is feasible, and then each campus team selects those, who will be in their program.

FAR MORE THAN A SCHOLARSHIP

Traditional scholarship programs dole out money if the student qualifies, and that is pretty much it. Call Me MISTER provides program participants with partial tuition assistance, but that assistance is more of an incentive for them to engage in a development process. What we need to see is some level of demonstrated commitment to teaching. If a candidate tells us that he wants to get into the program for the scholarship money, the financial rewards, or the support—and that is the extent of it—he is not going to make the cut.

Each candidate must understand that Call Me MISTER is a pathway to teaching at a lower-grade level in an elementary or middle school. He must be aware of that even if he does not fully comprehend what it entails. We do not expect the Misters entering the program to already be the people we will help them become.

Still, the candidates have to demonstrate evidence that they have already started on this journey in some meaningful way. Perhaps a young man has been a caretaker for his siblings, or he has shown service to children and youth in the community in some way: as a camp or peer counselor, for example, or as a teacher of Sunday school.

That is the kind of background we look for as evidence that the candidates have the propensity to serve the aims of Call Me MISTER. We ask them what they have been doing in life, what they are passionate about, what has inspired them, and what those experiences have meant to them. During such conversations, everything spills out. They lay it out right in front of us, and we can see the potential for wonderful teachers. The program takes it from there.

The program provides a number of benefits—tuition assistance, student support, and book allowance—once the candidate is accepted. It is not, however, a scholarship program. The commitment required is far deeper. The financial support offered by the program is meant merely to encourage these young men to pursue the calling to which they have dedicated themselves.

PEER SUPPORT

We recognize the importance of peer support in developing the Misters to their full potential. We have formally structured the program so that the Misters have to come into contact with one another. Typically, we recruit about five students per institution each year. We assign each cohort of Misters to a dormitory cluster or living learning community (LLC). They live together, they eat together, and they take the same classes. They move together through both their general education and, eventually, their professional courses.

Invariably, the Misters develop friendships. These friendships foster the peer identity and cultural development that is so important to the program's success. We want the Misters to be talking about education. We want them to be talking about teaching. We want them to be talking about their aspirations.

Feedback is an essential element of the program. Every week, we bring the Misters together to describe and discuss what has been going on with them in their studies, in their lives, and in the schools to which they are assigned. These young men receive mentoring through the program, including getting peer counseling from one another. Our counselors and advisors meet with the Misters individually, as well, and the Misters meet others in the program from other campuses during fall and spring summits. We want them to connect, whether such connection is through social networking, e-mailing, texting, blogging, making phone calls, or through any other methods by which they can stay in touch with others in the program.

SUMMER PROGRAMS

In addition, the program makes summer internships available at Clemson, for both the University's students, and those at other institutions. The students earn a very modest stipend for the internships, which include a two-month residential stint. During the Misters' four years of training, we encourage each to undergo at least one summer internship, where they are assigned daily to a site within a four county area working with a wide range of children and youth. These strategic partnerships allows Misters the opportunity to sharpen their personal and professional skills, while they are fully engaged with delivering enrichment activities to the target population.

Another of our co-curriculum's summer programs is the Call Me MISTER Leadership Institute. The Institute is an intense, focused, transformative, and engaging interaction among the participating Misters and our invited guest presenters, who have distinguished themselves as master teachers, engaged leaders, and accomplished authors and researchers. They raise the Misters' level of consciousness on a variety of relevant topics. Our distinguished presenters have included master teachers Salome Thomas-El and Hotep, Pulitzer Prize nominee and author Clifton Taulbert, professors James Anderson and Joy DeGruy, historian Vernon Burton, consultant Jawanza Kunjufu, and our honorary, inaugural institute presenter, Dr. David Williams.

Every Institute's closing session includes a presentation by professional Call Me MISTER teachers who are currently serving in South Carolina public schools. These sessions are powerfully inspiring and insightful, and they offer our prospective teachers a dose of the reality of life for the Misters serving fulltime in many of our most challenging schools.

AN EMPHASIS ON MENTORING

Mentoring is such a fundamental part of Call Me MISTER that it is incorporated into the program's name: The acronym stands for Mentors Instructing Students Toward Effective Role Models. Each of the Misters receives mentoring, and, in turn, each of them offers it in schools and community-based centers. Call Me MISTER is, therefore, a tri-level mentoring program that involves the program's professional mentors, the Misters learning to be mentors themselves, and the pupils to whom the Misters eventually reach out. We want the Misters to recognize that some of their students will need special attention outside the classroom, and that attention can be bestowed through tutoring and after-school programs. In such cases, mentoring plays a vital role.

We distinguish a mentor from a role model. A role model says, "Look at me, follow me, and do what I do." Everybody is a role model, for better or worse. A mentor, however, says, "You have it in you to be the best *you* can be." The mentor looks at the one he is helping and draws out unique talents, skills, and attributes. If you are a mentor, the focus is not on you during mentorship activities. Instead, it is on the one you are inspiring. You need a great deal of empathy, patience and understanding to be a mentor. A Mister, because of his background, has those qualities in abundance. Great teachers are great mentors—and great teaching and mentoring make a great Mister.

Teachers, by nature, are servant leaders. Their natural inclination is to be of service, and they are also in a leadership position in the classroom. Our philosophical objective is to develop teachers as servant leaders. You cannot be an effective teacher unless you have a real desire to be a servant; yet, you must lead as well, with the classroom as your domain. That is your charge. By serving, you lead—and by leading, you serve.

Our goal is to fulfill potential. The Call Me MISTER program is a laboratory, wherein these young men can make their mistakes and experience flashes of progress and change. It is where they can recognize their own abilities and what they can contribute. That is, what mentoring is all about.

IN THE WORDS OF THE MISTERS...

Lemanuel Chandler

"I am from a small area called Andrews but more close to a small community called Trio, South Carolina. My home is surrounded by trees and dirt roads. To this day, you can go back and see some of the old pavement that was done when I was a little boy; the pavement was of different colors and shapes of rocks.

"Because I was part of a family-oriented neighborhood, I spent most of my time around home, grandparents, great-aunts, and great-uncles. Although my parents had seven children altogether, only three of us grew up together—one being my twin brother and the other being my little sister who was two years younger.

"My first school was Head Start in Earls that is now closed. I remember the most loving teacher, Mrs. L. Nesmith, who would be there for me during accidents and hard times. I watched her spend time talking to my mom and trying to make the best of situations. I graduated and then went to D.P. Cooper Elementary. This school consisted of kindergarten to eighth grade. I felt good being at an elementary school with a band although there was never much more after that. I remember all my teachers from kindergarten until high school graduation.

"Of those teachers, seven of them met my need when I needed it most: Mrs. Paulette King, Mrs. Angela Rush, Mrs. Heather Sandra Lally, Mr. Wendell Williams, Mrs. D. Wright, Mrs. S. Cooper, and Mr. Allen Keels. However, teaching me to get through life were a janitor, Mr. Solomon Darby, and a bus driver, Mr. Harry Darby.

"After considering options, I chose to go to Clemson and major in special education. MISTER entered my life and met my biggest need. They have and will continue to save me from ignorance. In addition to Clemson, study abroad gave me the opportunity to go to the National University of Costa Rica.

"The people that I will remember most in life are Laura Ann Chandler, Inez Chandler, Aunt Virginia Darby, Solomon Darby, and Harry Darby, [all of whom] had a lot to do with my growth and [with the] development of my gift of music and how to live with people. Although the essential gifts or tenets of being a good person came from my parents, it took a village to make me who I am. My village was extended from Andrews to Clemson, to Orlando, and [then] to Costa Rica.

"Peers in my community always seemed better to me, being a young person. Most of my friends had basketball goals on the outside of their homes, four-wheelers to drive, [and] the newest video games, and [they] went places to shop for school. Although I'm grateful for what I've been blessed with, my parents' lifestyles always reminded me to be thankful and understand that things are not always what they seem like. Now that I'm older, I see the value in the words that they told us.

"The park in Trio and St. Lawrence was a place where members of the community used to come together and [where] all the children played together and learned together. When Boy Scouts got about three of us from the community, they later got all of us; that's how close our parents were. Now it's not the same; I don't see events like 'Save Our Young People' and 'Santee Social Club' and many more.

"Being away from home showed me another culture that I didn't know existed. Although we were always told that we could be anything we wanted to be, the words didn't have life in my culture. We were not able to see a college outside of the technical school that was in the area.

"I saw my first college when I came to Clemson University for orientation. I wanted to be a math teacher, so I enrolled as a teacher cadet and worked at Greeleyville Elementary during the summer. ... In high school... Mr. Hayward Jean did a presentation, and he was a Mister. He told stories and shared ideas about how to have great character in society and how gifts and talents are transferred to become great teachers and role models for others.

"Mrs. Angela Rush told me about the program and inspired me to learn as much as I can while I can. She told me that it was an opportunity that [could] change my life.

"In my K-12 experience, I would change the fact that a student would have to have an IEP [individualized education plan] to get help in reading and math. Once good teachers recognize an issue, I would want them to do what they can to satisfy the need. Recommending one [student] for service only allows time to go by while [another] one is continuing to fail. There were teachers who could have helped me but didn't because they didn't have to.

"I would also change the limited resources given to my school. Most of the students that did well at my school were students who visited the computer more [because they finished their work early or had some kind of personal relationship between the parent and the teacher]. Being able to do research on the computer was an asset in elementary school where I'm from. The most-liked students were given the better-looking books of the same edition. I remember getting a book that the previous student allowed a dog to chew on.

"The type of teacher I would like to become is one who advocates for students and the one who makes a difference in the world. I want to impact the lives of my students positively to the point that I give them 180 days but they allow me a lifetime to educate them. My 180 days would be given because it's mandated by the contract, but I want my students to give me more days because of who I was, what I gave them, and how my *being* gave them something to live for.

"The impact on the school would be less great than the impact in my classroom. My classroom is that lab in which I educate the whole child. The students will grow and develop to be great citizens at whom others can look as positive role models. I want to plant seeds in children, producing a crop of unprecedented success.

"MISTER is truly a lifestyle that is not for everyone. Although anyone can have it if they want it, it all starts with the mind and being willing to accept the fact that some of one's previous teachings were wrong. MISTER is not about reinventing the wheel. It has changed my life, and I've seen how it has changed so many other people's lives.

"MISTER is not about where you're from or where you currently stand; it's about where you're going and who you're going to be. This lifestyle has made me a lifelong member. I pray that I'm able to work in a MISTER office one day so I can give to many what I didn't have."

PART THREE

Spreading the Seeds

CHAPTER 1

Reaping What We Sow

In the 1967 film *In the Heat of the Night*, Sidney Poitier portrays Virgil Tibbs, a Philadelphia detective investigating a murder in the South. When a racist sheriff mocks Tibbs's name and asks what they call a boy like him back home, Poitier's character responds with a powerful retort: "They call me Mr. Tibbs." The line reflects his determination to live with dignity and respect.

This moment was our inspiration for naming the Call Me MISTER program, in which respect and reaching for dignity are key principles. Dr. Tom Parks, now a retired Clemson professor, coined the program name. At one time, under the Jim Crow laws, it was against the law to refer to a black man by his surname and the honorific "mister." The reference to *In the Heat of the Night* is apropos, but, in a deeper sense, it evokes a time in our history when black men were denied their very names.

We must remember that Jim Crow law was entrenched until the dawn of desegregation in schools: the *Briggs v. Elliot* case in Clarendon County, South Carolina, which led eventually to *Brown v. Board of Education*. So much of that mindset was used to try to justify lynchings. Many black men were hanged, not because they had committed some heinous crime, but because they had looked at a white woman or had not stepped off the curb. That led to Emmett

Till's fate. The fourteen-year-old, who came from Chicago, did not understand the rules, mores, and culture imposed upon black men in Mississippi. He looked too long and was crucified.

African Americans were compelled to navigate a dual consciousness. Imagine what it would be like to know yourself as a man of pride and dignity, yet find yourself uttering "Yes, sir" and "No, sir" to people who insist on calling you "boy." The lynchings were evil. So was the attempted assault on self-respect. While it is difficult to recall these atrocities, they are part of Southern history and must not be ignored during any process of healing these deep wounds inflicted on humanity.

REGAINING WHAT WAS LOST

Simultaneously, history must not ignore the unassailable truth that African Americans held tightly to respect and dignity in their homes and schools. The bonds of family and community helped them endure their pain. They found a context for happiness. When people live and die with principles and values, they define who they are as a people. When people cultivate respect, it grows in abundance.

That is what we are striving to regain through the Call Me MISTER program. Our teachers inspire respect. They must look and act like people worthy of following. We ask them to be conscious of their image; indeed, they dress well in public, and many wear suits to the classroom. However, this concept applies to far more than attire: It applies to attitude, disposition, and what Mister Mark Joseph often refers to as operating daily with a sense of purpose. All this is part of the Misters' image, and that becomes the cutting-edge difference. Do the Misters project themselves as individuals to whom people would entrust their children for teaching, regardless of race or background? We want the Misters to be able to walk into, any classroom, anywhere in the state, and hold their own.

That is what we are trying to build in the middle of challenges and barriers that can seem insurmountable. However, people must believe that things can change. The true solution lies in building communities. We want to plant the seeds for change so that hope and respect can flourish.

RECONNECTING WITH A STRONG PAST

Call Me MISTER recognizes that there are youth in our communities who have the potential to be teachers. People have come to assume that talent does not exist among wayward, misbehaving black boys, and they therefore overlook clear signs of potential and leadership. Once we identify talent, we can reconnect with the history that allowed communities to grow and build. We can reclaim our past dedication.

We had such dedication before the South was integrated. We all want to believe that integration was a plus for society, but we also need to recognize its downside: When schools were consolidated, and black and white children attended classes in the same buildings, the former black schools were closed down. Black teachers subsequently lost their jobs. Some left voluntarily, while others were forced out. Many found themselves lacking the necessary credentials and were demoted or relegated to much lesser duties. A principal who served a black school in the 1960s may have found himself serving as the bus duty supervisor or janitorial manager a decade later at a consolidated school.

It happened often. Men who had served as clear role models in their communities lost that professional status and strength. At the same time, communities began to lose the values that these teachers and administrators had helped to instill in students. You could see the changes even in the ways students dressed and talked.

The impact on black communities was significant. Many of today's young people do not recognize what has happened. Call Me MISTER works to show them a strong tradition. The program seeks to reinstate those role models by introducing a new wave of great black educators.

A NEW CROP OF MENTORS

A Mister is a teacher in the fullest sense. He does not see teaching as a 7:30 a.m. to 3:00 p.m. job; instead, he sees it as a commitment to complete student development. He wants to advance from being the student who is mentored to become a mentor for his own students. He wants to develop others' talents, skills, and virtues. He wants to guide and transform lives.

A Mister does not write anybody off. He is not discouraged because a child comes to school ill-prepared, dirty, hungry, or disheveled. He accepts a child, whether that child looks like him or not, or whether that child has an entirely different background or not. That must be a Mister's attitude and demeanor, or he cannot hope to connect with kids or see their potential.

In short, a Mister must be dedicated to sowing respect. If people give respect, they find that they soon will get it in return. We must restore an aura of respect in our communities because it is fundamental to growth and development.

Respect, however, must be planted and nurtured. It is harder to assess than the test scores that measure student achievement, yet it has everything to do with that achievement. If properly cultivated, what we sow can yield a great harvest of human potential.

CHAPTER 2

The Vision Widens

For its first several years, Call Me MISTER was primarily a South Carolinian program involving Clemson, Benedict, Claflin, Morris and eventually, South Carolina State. Between 2005 and 2007, we began to expand within the state and started to include other two-year technical colleges and other four-year colleges. That expansion has continued, reaching today's total of 15 institutions in the state.

In 2007, we began to expand outside South Carolina. We achieved this expansion through the development of a licensing agreement between Clemson and other colleges and universities, thereby launching an initiative for Call Me MISTER. Through this licensing, the program falls under the umbrella of each partner institution.

Before an institution can be licensed, we require consultations and two-day site visits. Call Me MISTER staff members, sometimes accompanied by program Misters, visit the institution to make sure its representatives understand and are committed to the program and the integrity of the brand. We make sure we are all on the same page.

At that point, our licensing office issues the agreement, which allows the new partner institution to use our trademark name of Call Me MISTER, along with the logo and tool-kit of materials. The licensing agreement lays out the details of our commitment and the timeline.

We initiated the licensing process to protect our brand and trademark. We did not want to see Call Me MISTER associated with commercial endeavors unrelated to the program's mission.

A NATIONAL REACH

Through our licensing efforts, the program has grown steadily, reaching eight other states and the District of Columbia. As of this writing, 25 universities are involved. The Southeast is the primary geographical region, but we reach as far north as Pennsylvania and as far west as Missouri.

When we launched as a South Carolina program in 2000, we did not intend that Call Me MISTER would become a national program. We did state from the very start that we felt the model had the potential to be replicated nationally. While that was in our literature from the start, that was not really our intention.

Instead, we wanted to consolidate and solidify the development of Call Me MISTER, within South Carolina, to address a South Carolina problem. Many of those involved in the program did not believe the program should reach beyond the state. In fact, most did not believe the program should go beyond the original partners. People simply expected Call Me MISTER would remain a collaboration and partnership between Clemson and the historically black colleges.

We began to get feedback from people throughout the state that it was a great idea; others wanted to know how they could become involved. The Clemson faithful wondered why the University did not have any Misters on its campus. We, simply, did not have a mechanism for others to become involved. We realized that we needed a statewide strategy, which we started developing in about 2005.

THE TRUE MEASURE OF GROWTH

The growth of our program is more about quality than about numbers. We could try to measure the development and success of Call Me MISTER in terms of the number of recruits, graduates, and teaching placements. We could count how many Misters have been named teacher of the year. We do our best to ensure that the Misters develop from freshmen to seniors to graduates. Yet all of those facts do not begin to tell the story.

The true measure of Call Me MISTER comes over the long haul, as young men come into the program, develop their service leadership acumen, and take their experiences into classrooms. Through this process, we have begun to see the significant impact that Mister teachers have on their students' development and achievements.

That is the measure of growth we see in competent, effective, and enthusiastic teachers learning to tell their stories and share their heritage. That growth is what is behind the Call Me MISTER brand. Our brand is rooted in the experiences of students, families, and communities. In the final analysis, the program's evaluation will depend on how well we are able to serve and empower them.

CHAPTER 3

Where Next?

What is the future for Call Me MISTER and the teachers it prepares for service? When we put that question to Mister Hayward Jean, he responded, "The sky's the limit."

If we continue to receive support from the resources it takes to expand and scale up, then the program's possibilities indeed seem limitless. The program can certainly spread nationwide, as it has already begun to do.

We have remained true to our mission in finding native sons where they stand and then broadening their vision, so in turn they can honor their families, schools, and communities through their great work.

A DEMONSTRATED NEED

We have demonstrated that the need is out there. We ourselves have not initiated the expansion thus far. The reason we have expanded into several other states is that the institutions in those states have solicited us to launch the program and develop a Call Me MISTER partnership. Each semester since 2005, somebody has reached out to us, asking whether we might expand.

Strategically, our priority is the South. We feel a commitment to not only South Carolina but to the region, so we want expansion to be primarily in the Southern states, although we have made inroads elsewhere. We do have limitations of resources and human power. We have managed this growth with the same core staff we started with years ago. Our full-time staff has not increased at all. We have only added temporary workers here and there to ensure liaison support at various colleges and universities.

Our program has shown itself to be an answer—not necessarily *the* answer—to a common set of problems nationwide: the shortage of African American male teachers and the dismal academic performance of African American male students. The widespread issue also includes Latinos, Native Americans, Asians and other students of color.

Our phone rings regularly with callers describing the same problem. They tell us they have heard about us and would like to see a Call Me MISTER initiative in their area. They have seen our success, and they do not want to reinvent the wheel. That idea gets the conversation started, but those who come to us must also be able to bring resources to the table. At this point, we do not have a national source of support for expansion.

TREASURE IN OUR BACKYARDS

Still, as we move forward into a promising yet uncertain future, we know we are on the right track. Traditional approaches to education have continued to leave behind so many young children, especially black males. The traditional approach to recruiting and retaining teachers basically starts with the assumption that only certain people are destined to be teachers, especially teachers in elementary schools.

Many teachers are not the first in their families to pursue the career. They usually come from families of teachers.

Even in South Carolina, where a third of the student body is African American, less than 15 percent of the teachers are African American. Of those few who are men, most teach at the secondary level. There has long been an established pipeline for teachers, and that pipeline has not encouraged black males to teach at the elementary level. Yet, it is in early childhood that formal development and student achievement truly begin. Of those students who do not do well, most begin to falter as early as the first few years of elementary school.

A teacher's background, culture, and race do make a difference. Any child, black or white, who never had a black man as a teacher in the early grades will carry a perception of what a teacher is and should be, and what a teacher is not and should not be. A teacher might promote academic achievement and excellence, or insist on standards and accountability, but the pupil may not hear it. "My teacher doesn't look or talk like me," the pupil reasons, "so that stuff's not for me." How a black boy perceives a teacher "feels" about him, predisposes how that child will perform for him or her, which very well may be the most underrated factor of all. He begins to slip. He fails to read or do arithmetic at grade level. By fourth or fifth grade, he is in trouble. That is why Call Me MISTER focuses on the lower grades.

We firmly believe that the answer to the problem lies right in our own backyards. A treasure of talent is buried there, and our program is able to mine it. A young man from a rural black community or small town might never otherwise consider teaching, even though he has the aptitude and heart for such a career. Without encouragement, he will be overlooked or skipped. Call Me MISTER gives him reason to believe that someone like him has something to contribute. It assures him of his value, and it brings the potential to fruition.

WHEREVER OUR MISSION LEADS US

The program works the same way everywhere with the same philosophy. The idea is not equivalent to thinking, "We need Washington to come in and fix us." Communities take ownership of their own problems. At times, school districts have looked outside of the country to find teachers who will work in South Carolina. That is nothing short of ridiculous. If people truly respect and honor their own community and state, they need not look far to find good teacher candidates.

Call Me MISTER will continue to find, train, develop, and launch these candidates into communities where they can make a difference. The talent, and the potential, is right in front of us.

This is the same message we are taking to Mississippi, Virginia, Kentucky, Florida, Georgia, and Pennsylvania. It is the same message we will be taking wherever our mission leads us in the years ahead.

IN THE WORDS OF THE MISTERS...

Aaron Cokley

"I grew up with a single mother, and I have three other siblings. We struggled. We were on welfare—I remember we used the stove for heat. We ate Kaboom cereal and government cheese, and we were not able to buy certain items in the grocery store. We struggled, but my mom was very motivated. My mom finished high school and her first job was with Dunkin' Donuts.

"I got a job to help around the house. My mom was a single parent and I knew she couldn't buy things that I wanted or needed, but I understood that, and I got a job on my own account. I worked at BI-LO—and, oh, my goodness, they had me do everything! I did bag boy, produce, dairy, [and] stocking. Just having that job gave me [the] motivation that I wanted something better in life. I did this while in high school and I ran track, played tennis, and played drums and trumpet in the marching band. I also did praise and worship at my church. I led songs on praise team.

"My guidance counselor wasn't very encouraging. I would take information to him, and he would always push me to technical school. My grades were good—I had a 3.9, but I had never taken honors courses. I never had the guidance counselor sit down and tell me, 'You need to do this and this' to go to a four-year university. I never had this until my senior year, which was already too late.

"I felt lost in a sense, like Moses in the wilderness. It was heartbreaking to tell my family that because I didn't take certain courses I couldn't go to a four-year university. I had one teacher, a black male coach named Harvey Mack, and he pushed me. He told me, 'You can do this.' He told me to apply to a four-year university anyway.

"[Later, when I was at the university] I was an RA on campus, and Michael Barron, a Mister, was an RA. I noticed how he dressed, how he spoke. I thought he was a business major. I spoke to him and he told me that he was an education major, and I [thought], *'Wow!'* I'd never seen a teacher dress the way he did. He wore a coat and tie every day, and I mean every day. I was impressed with that. I asked him why he dressed up if he wasn't in the classroom now. He said, well, he was preparing for where he was going. He always wowed me!

"The best teachers learn with their students. Teachers must connect with students to induce, to draw out from within those golden nuggets: the nuggets that help the students to see how great they are. They must also be able to tie curriculum with real-world experience.

"When I'm a teacher that's what I'll do. I have to; I have no choice. I must do it because there are other Aarons out there.

"I'm going into deaf education [and] sign language. MISTER gave me that. MISTER helped me define my niche. I majored in elementary education while I found my niche. I'm going to Gallaudet University in Washington, D.C., to get my master's in deaf education. It is so good to find your niche…so good! I plan to come back to South Carolina and teach and fulfill my promise to MISTER!"

═══════════════════════════════

CONCLUSION

"Teamwork Makes the Dream Work"

The Call Me MISTER commitment to caring is all-encompassing. The Misters are on a mission to save children—the white children as well as the black. That is what they tell us. That is the spirit of caring they embrace.

Children of any race, ethnicity, or background need to love themselves and be proud of their people. To do so, they must understand their story. They need to know who they are, where they came from, and what the values that sustained their forebears are. That is true whether the child is black or white, Hispanic or Irish, or whether the child is Jewish, Christian, or Muslim.

The Misters in our program are dedicated to appreciating differences in people and to working together for the good of all. They take to heart the program's motto: "Teamwork Makes the Dream Work." Today, the young men who are embarking on the Call Me MISTER mission were small children themselves when we inaugurated the program. Their dreams were in the process of being born. Now we have found these dreamers—or they have found us.

Some feel the calling early, and others develop it by witnessing passion in others. One young man was playing college football when he first heard about Call Me MISTER. He had not thought about being a teacher before that. A professor brought the program to his attention, and the young man attended a summer institute. What sold him on the idea of teaching, he told us, was the experience of being around other young black men who were so passionate about helping children. That changed him.

A CROP OF MASTER TEACHERS

We are dedicated to the development of master teachers. Master teachers are those who have committed to mastering their content and perfecting the art of teaching, so that they can be the most effective educators and leaders possible. They have learned to connect with students, and they do so in a way that helps those students achieve. A central element is this: A master teacher cannot separate himself from his role as mentor. He must be able to share his own story. By doing so, he helps himself grow, and he also can help others grow.

In the classroom, a teacher will encounter a diversity of children with stories similar to and different from his own; to be an effective mentor, he must know how to respond to all of them. Vicarious experience is effective in reaching children who are going through a wide variety of challenges.

A teacher must be able to empower others to overcome their circumstances. When a child needs help, a teacher has no time to wait for a policy to change. A teacher has no time to wait for the school district to hire a different principal or superintendent or to hope for something better in the next election. That child needs a teacher who will not be slow to reach out with a helping hand and a helping heart.

A teacher of such high quality means the world to the pupils fortunate enough to have one. Out of their appreciation and respect, they well might begin to see a vision for themselves: Perhaps, one day, they could be teachers too.

After all, a boy aspires to be a man; if a teacher is of his own race and culture, the student can more readily identify with that man. Day after day, that child will see a man who cares. This sight is a powerful antidote to the violent imagery from the mouths of many rap stars—and for lack of a better role model, many children come to idolize these rappers, whom, most likely, they have never seen in person. How much better it would be if children could look up to teachers who offer and require respect. How much better it would be if children wanted to do what they observed their teachers doing. In such a manner, the seeds are planted.

Humble, respectful, caring, and stable. Those can be the attributes of children who are nurtured by such teachers. Those are attributes that run contrary to the stereotypes about black youth. We know these young people will bring stability to their communities—and that sense of stability, in time, can become a community's norm.

THE CONTEXT OF COMMUNITY

Each Mister has to recognize that a child comes to the classroom in a context of siblings, peers, immediate and extended family, community, church, and neighborhood. All of these factors have an impact on that child's emotions, mindset, and behavior.

Nearly all of the Misters, who have gone through the program, have had more than just a passing relationship with the families of the children they serve in their classrooms. They forge connections with the families, which is an important dimension of their service. It is also important for the Mister to know whether that family is supportive or needs help in becoming supportive. Each Mister recognizes that there are multiple stakeholders involved in determining whether that child is going to be successful or not.

Each person's story is different from the next person's story, whether that story is good, bad, better, or worse. We live among a diverse population, with diverse experiences. As teachers begin to hear stories, they learn to assess the situations at home. Some parents may feel insecure about their educational levels. They may be a little ashamed or embarrassed. Maybe, they cannot read well.

A teacher must be discerning of and sensitive to ways of helping each family. To do so, he must be comfortable with community culture. A teacher needs to be able to sit down and eat with the people he hopes to help. He needs to be able to roll up his sleeves and get in there with the families. We do not rely on one semester of student teaching to instill that kind of mindset. Instead, we foster that mindset during the years of development Call Me MISTER offers.

As we write, more than eighty Misters have graduated with full credentials, and about one hundred forty are in the pipeline in South Carolina alone. They head out to be advocates for children and to build supportive communities. Their approach must be fearless.

Some of the Misters have become principals and gone on to pursue advanced degrees. They give every indication that they will become the state's educational leaders. They are becoming powerful agents of change. Ultimately, if Call Me MISTER has its way, it will offer South Carolina and the nation a brilliant group of black men, who will serve as guides, leading the way to stronger families and communities.

RESTORING A POSITION OF HONOR

In this way, Call Me MISTER is helping to restore the role that teachers traditionally played in African American culture. Teachers and preachers were the undeniable stalwarts in the community.

As these roles have fragmented, as families have broken down and communities have become blighted, a downward spiral of despair has set in. How can that be reversed? We are contributing to this reversal by committing to reaffirming, reestablishing, and reclaiming the pride and honor of black men in becoming teachers. We find young men who are rooted in their communities and, who will stand firm in helping to develop those communities.

Once, black teachers and principals were the norm in African American communities. Schoolmates and their parents and teachers went to church together. Schools were so rooted in their communities that the same senior teacher might have taught generations of the same family.

As Fairclough observed: "Whether their classrooms were in red-brick, Gothic-towered universities or ram-shackled schoolhouses of rough-sawn planks, teachers saw themselves as leaders of the race and considered themselves, to use modern parlance, role models."

It was a culture of accountability. Children knew that their teachers had control over them, and that they must give them the respect due their elders or face family, extended family or community consequences, not jail houses. To this day, some people feel that the downfall of the schools came from outlawing corporal punishment or from taking prayer away. When teachers had real authority, there was nowhere a child could run and hide. The teacher was like another parent.

Do you think a twenty-two-year-old white female views herself that way—as a second parent to a ten-year-old black child, who is acting out? Is she thinking at all along those lines? Absolutely not. Is it her fault? Absolutely not. She comes out of her own family tradition and out of a teacher-training program that did not instruct her about the cultural connection needed to reach the most at-risk kids from low-income backgrounds. She is not prepared for that. She was not oriented. It was not an expectation.

As we have made abundantly clear in this book, African Americans have long had a sense of ownership regarding schools: They ran their schools themselves, both public and private. They were teachers, disciplinarians, and administrators. That changed as the nation, and particularly the South, evolved from segregation to integration and then to school consolidation. By the early 1970s, well after *Brown v. Board of Education* and the Civil Rights Act, black and white kids were going to school together. Yet, at the same time, consolidation cost the black community its schools.

African Americans lost autonomy over education. For the sake of integration, they lost leadership over their schools, and they lost personnel; the black men and women who had been teachers. School leaders, if they stayed, were relegated to lower status. Teacher quality and dedication suffered. No longer did a teacher stand in front of the classroom thinking, "That's my child I'm teaching."

How can we turn this around? There's no silver bullet. People place great hope in technology, but it is a tool, not an answer. The answers lie in our own humanity, in cultural memory, and in being proud of a history that shows African Americans stood tall. They built vibrant and stable communities. We must restore awareness and faith in their history. We must restore the role of teacher as a position of honor.

GIVING BACK

Communities have lost so much. The best talent has fled, looking someplace else for answers. For decades, African Americans have tended to migrate, seeking better pastures in Charlotte, Atlanta, and Washington, D.C. The irony is that they themselves were the answers, and they took those answers away from their people. Once-thriving communities now seem barren.

The people left behind often are worse off for having lost someone, who would have contributed to their community. Those who leave may not give a second thought to how that community will fight for itself. If they do come home again, they are likely to find their old friends and neighbors—and their families—in even more distress.

Survival is not good enough. It is time to do more than just get through the day. For long-term healing, new energy will flow through communities, if the best and the brightest stay put. We can replace the downward spiral of despair with an upward spiral of hope. People will no longer feel that someone needs to save them. Instead of always looking for entitlements, they can find empowerment. They can find their own potential. That goes to the core of the Call Me MISTER mission—to draw out the potential of bright young people to give back to their communities, rather than flee and further drain the talent.

The solution is to instill in youth the value of investing in their communities, of rebuilding, and of fighting. We want to see a new generation of people who say, "My sleeves are rolled up, and I'm here." We want to see young people who want to give back.

Each of us may recall a teacher we knew, someone who influenced us deeply—and then was gone. We felt a keen sense of loss. It is time for communities to fight a very similar sense of loss. This is not some romantic notion of sitting in a circle singing "Kumbaya", so we will all live happily ever after. The intent is clear: We will take ownership and do something about what has hurt us.

That is the thrust of the Call Me MISTER program. The Misters come from a deep-rooted legacy of teachers in a community that has valued them. These young men were destined to be where they are today. The challenge they face might seem hopeless. It is not. Once the problems are recognized, once the problems are in the open, hope can enter. There is opportunity for growth.

We see that hope shining clearly in our program. The good news is in the sparkle of a Mister's eyes, in his energy and his enthusiasm for what the future can hold. Many are young men of strong faith, and though they may lack confidence at the start, they attain it. Some gain it more quickly than others, and some simply do not come from a tradition of trust. We ask them to give it a try with us, and we travel together. We can make it through, and we can give back.

THE TRUE TEST

How have the Misters fared? A significant number of them have become "teachers of the year"—and they have attained that distinction quickly. The feedback from schools, parents, and communities indicates that the Misters are making a difference. They have graduated from our institutions and headed out into the field, and they have stuck and stayed. Since the program's inception more than a decade ago, not one Mister among our graduates in South Carolina have left the profession. Some have become administrative leaders.

The Misters have, in other words, stood the true test of what makes a great teacher, even if their students still struggle. They are making a difference in ways that can be hard to measure. Some of our graduates are in tougher schools than others. Some face greater challenges in getting their pupils to perform and in helping hurting communities. If a Mister can lead a class from one year to the next and show growth among students, who once appeared hopelessly behind, that is highly significant, even if the performance does not quite hit standards. The trajectory cannot be ignored; in time, the Misters' work will hit the mark and exceed it.

What matters is commitment. Whether or not a Mister feels counter to the prevailing culture of an area, what matters is his ability to reach out to young people and families. That is the primary objective of our program. Those in the educational system—no matter their background, race, or gender—who are champions for kids will feel no division between "us" and "them." The objectives of Call Me MISTER, align with the objectives of anyone, who is an advocate and champion for all young people. If someone acts counter to the culture of caring, then he or she should not be in the teaching profession.

For the Misters, the art of teaching will embrace the stories of who African Americans are as a people: the good, the bad, and the ugly. That is where the teachers develop their art—beyond the content. That is how they connect. The ability to do so is the most valuable attribute that the Misters—and all teachers—can bring to the profession, if they hope to be effective and enhance learning and growth. If a person does not have the ability to connect with students, then he or she will not have the ability to teach them anything.

This is an old-school philosophy that describes the history of black education in the South, which is one of interacting with the students, families, and communities. As a teacher who is dedicated to that philosophy, a Mister is not just walking into a classroom to take on a job. He is committed to a mission that is bigger than himself.

Misters understand that. They are spreading seeds with the expectation that those seeds will take root and flourish and that the crop will ripen in the sun. They want to do more than produce enough to just get by, year to year. They want to help sustain children, families, and communities for generations, and they are preparing the ground for a bountiful harvest.

The Call Me MISTER student vision statement captures the essence of the spirit that drives the program—and the men whom it sends out to communities that so badly need them:

"I am a dedicated servant leader who is perpetuating a sorely needed concept: servant leaders as role models in elementary schools. I am devoted to planting seeds of dignity and respect in children and inspiring them to cultivate those seeds, producing a crop of unprecedented success. I will teach reading, writing, and arithmetic and progress to self-esteem, imagination, and determination.

"Because of my immeasurable promise, not only have I earned your respect, I demand it! A title is only important if one's character and integrity dictate its use. When you address me, please verbalize my destiny. Please do not call me by my first name. Call me in reference to my great vision—call me MISTER!"

IN THE WORDS OF THE MISTERS...

Steven Stokes

"When I read the vision statement of Call Me MISTER, I saw that it was much more than academics. It was about becoming better people in society.

"In the neighborhood that I grew up in, I saw people who had potential but had no one to encourage them, so they ended up not reaching their potential. A lot of them went into a life of criminality."

Micquan Roberts

"I was brought up in a town where my grandmama lived because my mom worked and my dad worked, so we would have to go to my grandmama's house. My grandmama's neighborhood is where most of the violence went on. Gangs were there. We weren't bothered, but we still heard gunshots and all that type of stuff. I guess we just couldn't get away from it. I was never involved with anything myself, but in the town there were always murders going on, people killing people, and people breaking in. I'll never forget one time at the store in front of my grandmama's house—and this is the store we always went to, you know, for snacks and stuff—we heard someone using a sledgehammer or something trying to break in the door. He would hit it for a while, then he would go away, [and] then he would come back, and he kept trying to break in. He never actually got in, though, because the glass was too strong. I remember that like it was yesterday—someone trying to break in the store that we [would] go to every day.

"The jobs in my town would be jobs that you really didn't want–jobs that would be okay for people in high school. My mom, all she had were different plant jobs. Now my dad, he mostly worked out of town; they were plant jobs, but they were better than what my mom had. The job opportunities, actually, in Dillon, aren't too good. When people there get hired for some of those plants, it's lovely, because of the money; they're not used to it. And it seems like they are good jobs, but they actually are not. The job opportunities are not so good there.

"I started working in my ninth-grade year, and I worked all four years in high school. My first job was at a family grocery. My next job was [at a] another grocery store, and my next job was [at] McDonald's. My last job in high school was [at] KFC. My parents gave me what I needed, but I wanted my own job so I could provide for myself.

"My only African American teacher was my band teacher; [the teachers of] my core classes were all women, all white women, and I think, finally, I had a black female teacher in sixth grade and I had a black female teacher in ninth grade.

"Dr. [Ronald] Speight [collaborator for Call Me MISTER at South Carolina State] and I have a really close relationship now. He is always there. He is always pushing us to do better and better than what we are [achieving]; even though he tells us things and we might not want to hear [them], we still think about [them]. I know he is there and behind us 100 percent."

Derrick Blanding

"In my senior year at Pendleton High School, Mister Justin Ballenger told me about Call Me MISTER. I took it upon myself to befriend some of the other Misters. I learned that it would be a valuable brotherhood organization to grow in, and it has become really much more than that.

"TEAMWORK MAKES THE DREAM WORK"

"The network that we have built is almost indescribable!"

MISTERS WHO SELFLESSLY ALLOWED US TO COME INTO THEIR LIVES BY SHARING THEIR STORIES

Michael Hopkins
Brandon McIntosh
Marquice Clarke
Daniel Groves
Kwadjo Campbell
Keith Wilkes
Thomas Cayruth
Lemanuel Chandler
Aaron Cokley
Steven Stokes
Micquan Roberts
Derrick Blanding

ACADEMIC COACHES: THE TEAM THAT MAKES THE DREAM WORK EACH AND EVERY DAY!

Dr. Beverly McAdams, Anderson University
Anthony Broughton, Benedict College
Kendrick Cherry, Claflin University
Dr. Jerome Christia, Coastal Carolina University
Floyd Breeland, Renard Harris, College of Charleston
Rudy Wheeler, Morris College
Dr. Reggie Wicker, John Lesaine, Newberry College
Dr. Ronald Speight, South Carolina State University
Harvey Choplin, Southern Wesleyan University
Larry Jackson, University of South Carolina – Beaufort
Richard Dawkins, Greenville Technical College
Paul Livingston, Midlands Technical College

Dr. Gwen Owens, Tri-County Technical College
William Wrighten, Trident Technical College

CALL ME MISTER HEADQUARTERS

Dr. Roy Jones, Executive Director
Winston Holton, Field Coordinator
James Lindsey, Program Coordinator
Tanya Miller, Administrative Assistant
Allen Friend, Program Support
Wayne Wright, Community Volunteer Team

CLEMSON

The Infrastructure of Support that Makes the Day-to-Day Operation of the Program Possible, Particularly:

Dr. Dori Helms, Provost
Dr. Lawrence Allen, Dean

The Faculty & Staff of the Eugene T. Moore School of Education, **Neil Cameron**, Vice President for Institutional Advancement (Marketing Guru Extraordinaire) and the staff of the Development Office, **Harrison "Hack" Trammell**, President, Clemson University Foundation and its Board, **Catherine Sams**, Director and the Staff of the Public Affairs Office, **Vincie Albritton** and the Clemson University Research Foundation, **JoAnna Floyd** and the Clemson University Licensing and Contracts Office. Also, special thanks to **Dr. Lamont Flowers, Dr. Lienne Medford, Dot Moss, Msiba Dalton, Dr. Suzanne Rosenblith, Dr. Rob Knoeppel, Dr. Janie Lindle**, and retirees **Pat Padgett** and **Dr. Bill Fisk** for their help in making the journey much smoother to navigate.

SUMMER INTERNSHIP COMMUNITY ENGAGEMENT PARTNERS

Littlejohn Community Center
Project Middle Passage
Emerging Scholars
Easley Housing Authority
Toxaway United Methodist Church camp
Blue Ridge Elementary School Club Leap
King David Baptist Church Jump Start
A Unique Homework Center

MAJOR DONORS & SUPPORTERS

To our current and past foundation and corporate donors, who provided funding support, along with their belief and confidence that Call Me MISTER was the right idea to support.

BMW Automobile Manufacturer
Charles Stewart Mott Foundation
Dabo and Kathleen Swinney's All In Foundation
Duke Energy Foundation
Dupont Corporation
Lumina Foundation's McCabe Fund
Michelin Corporation
Oprah's Angel Network
Self Family Foundation
State of South Carolina Legislature
Sunshine Lady Foundation
Wachovia Foundation (now Wells Fargo)
Wells Fargo Foundation
W.K. Kellogg Foundation

SUPPLIER OF THE CALL ME MISTER BLAZER SINCE 2004

Gregory's Boutique of Greer & Greenville, South Carolina

OTHER STATES WITH COLLEGES LICENSED TO HOST A CALL ME MISTER INITIATIVE

Virginia (Longwood University)

Kentucky (Eastern Kentucky University)

Florida (University of Phoenix - Jacksonville, Edward Waters College)

Mississippi (Jackson State University)

District of Columbia (Gallaudet University)

Georgia (Georgia College)

Pennsylvania (Cheyney University)

Missouri (Metropolitan Community College - Penn Valley)

CALL ME MISTER HONOR ROLL OF GRADUATES

Donald Amis
Rashad Anderson
Justin Ballenger
Micheal Barron
Derrick Blanding
Cameron Brice
Anthony Broughton
Tremelle Brown
Derrick Butler
Jaron Cannon
Lemanuel Chandler
Kendrick Cherry
Marquice Clark
Brack Clemmons
Wallace Cobbs
Aaron Cokley
Peter Commodore
Farroll Daniels
Everett Davis
Randy Dendy
Zebulun Dinkins
David Fair
Dwayne Fludd
Jimmy Freeman
Lorenzo Gaines
Nicholas Gillcrese
Demetrius Green
Quinton Gregory

William Handy
Jared Holloway
Timothy Hughes
Hayward Jean
Howard Jean
Tyrone Jefferson
Edward Johnson
Mark Joseph
Mansa Joseph
Herbert Joyner
Demeturia Kelly
David Kelly
Walter Lee
Eric Lewis
Andrew Little
Willie S. Lynch
Ernest Mackins
Brandon McIntosh
Brandon Middleton
LeAndrea Montgomery
Andre' Moss
Rashad Myers
DaWayne Nettles
Lawrence Ochieng
Thomas Odom
Marcus Peel-Cooke
Damon Qualls
Quentin Ramsey

Eric Richardson
Ricardo Robinson
Thomas Savage
Sterling Savage
Leon Scott
Daniel Spencer
Michael Spencer
Larrell Spurgeon
Breslin Steverson
Antonio Taylor
Marvin Taylor
Cory Terry
Cedric Thompson
Sherod Thurman
Thomas Turner
Jamario Twitty
Amos Walker
AbdurRabb Watkins
Tony Webb, Jr.
Keith Wilkes
Brian Williams
Jayuntay Williams
Sherman Williams
Terrence Wilson
Robert Wilson

How can you use this book?

MOTIVATE

EDUCATE

THANK

INSPIRE

PROMOTE

CONNECT

Why have a custom version of *Call Me MISTER*?

- Build personal bonds with customers, prospects, employees, donors, and key constituencies
- Develop a long-lasting reminder of your event, milestone, or celebration
- Provide a keepsake that inspires change in behavior and change in lives
- Deliver the ultimate "thank you" gift that remains on coffee tables and bookshelves
- Generate the "wow" factor

Books are thoughtful gifts that provide a genuine sentiment that other promotional items cannot express. They promote employee discussions and interaction, reinforce an event's meaning or location, and they make a lasting impression. Use your book to say "Thank You" and show people that you care.

Call Me MISTER is available in bulk quantities and in customized versions at special discounts for corporate, institutional, and educational purposes. To learn more please contact our Special Sales team at:

1.866.775.1696 • sales@advantageww.com • www.AdvantageSpecialSales.com

CPSIA information can be obtained at www.ICGtesting.com
Printed in the USA
LVOW132351030113

314302LV00002B/2/P